IN THE TEETH OF THE WIND

IN THE TEETH OF THE WIND

The Story of a Naval Pilot
on the Western Front
1916–1918

by
Squadron Leader
C.P.O. Bartlett DSC★

Edited by his son,
Nick Bartlett

Pen & Sword
MILITARY

First published in 1974
by Ian Allan Ltd

Published in 2004
and re-printed in this format in 2013 by

Pen & Sword Military
an imprint of
Pen & Sword Books Ltd
47 Church Street
Barnsley
South Yorkshire
S70 2AS

The right of C.P.O. Bartlett to be identified as author of this work has
been asserted by him in accordance with the Copyright, Designs and
Patents Act 1988.

ISBN:- 978-1-78346-181-3

Printed and bound in the UK by CPI Group (UK) Ltd, Croydon, CRO 4YY

Pen & Sword Books Ltd incorporates the Imprints of Pen & Sword Aviation,
Pen & Sword Family History, Pen & Sword Maritime, Pen & Sword Military, Pen
& Sword Discovery, Wharncliffe Local History, Wharncliffe True Crime,
Wharncliffe Transport, Pen & Sword Select, Pen & Sword Military Classics, Leo
Cooper, The Praetorian Press, Remember When, Seaforth Publishing
and Frontline Publishing.

For a complete list of Pen & Sword titles please contact
PEN & SWORD BOOKS LIMITED
47 Church Street, Barnsley, South Yorkshire, S70 2AS, England
E-mail: enquiries@pen-and-sword.co.uk
Website: www.pen-and-sword.co.uk

CONTENTS

Glossary

AA	Anti-Aircraft
AM	Air Mechanic
Archie	Nickname for anti-aircraft fire, from contemporary music hall catch-phrase, "Archibald, certainly not!"
Bessoneau(x)	French design of aircraft field hangar, of canvas roof and sides, with bulky wooden internal framework
CMB	Central Medical Board (in London)
CPO	Chief Petty Officer, Royal Navy
DH	DH4 bomber
DO	Duty Officer
EA	Common abbreviation for enemy aircraft
F/Cdr	Flight Commander (RNAS rank)
F/Lt	Flight Lieutenant (RNAS rank)
F/S/Lt	Flight Sub-Lieutenant (RNAS rank)
HE	High Explosive
KB	Kite Balloon
Lower Deck	Naval Term for non-commissioned ratings
Mufti	Civilian clothes
PBI	Poor Bloody Infantry
Napoo	Useless or non-existent
PO	Petty Officer, Royal Navy
RFC	Royal Flying Corps
RNAS	Royal Naval Air Service
RNVR	Royal Naval Volunteer Reserve
USAS	United States Air Service

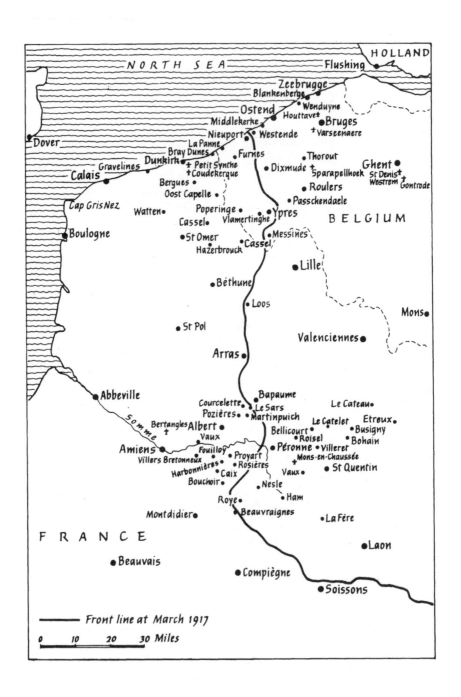

Front line at March 1917

0   10   20   30 Miles

Introduction

In July, 1914, when at Churchill's instigation the British Admiralty's Air Department was formed into the Royal Naval Air Service, the intention was that its work would be solely to support the Navy. Yet, within weeks of its first squadron arriving in France, RNAS units equipped with armoured cars were skirmishing against the flank of the German army in its advance on Antwerp. Next, at the request of the French, an RNAS seaplane base was established at Dunkirk as a contribution to the defence of the threatened port, and from there a number of spectacular raids were made on Zeppelin sheds as far away as Cologne, Düsseldorf and Cuxhaven — notable achievements considering the very primitive aircraft and navigational aids available in 1914.

As the protagonists gradually settled down to trench warfare it became obvious that a huge traffic of men and war material across the Channel would need to be sustained and given the strongest possible protection, the task being given to Vice Admiral Sir Reginald Bacon's forces, known as the Dover Patrol. One of its components were the several RNAS squadrons based on aerodromes around Dunkirk.

By the historic resistance of remnants of the small Belgian Army and the opening of the dykes, the German advance on Dunkirk, threatening Calais and Boulogne too, was held near Dixmude, 15 miles to the east. By the end of the year the persistence of British and Belgian troops, fighting in the appalling flooded trenches along the valley of the Yser, had secured an anchorage for the left flank of the 180-mile Allied front which held firm for the rest of the war. The ports of Ostende, Bruges and Zeebrugge, being in German hands, however, posed a constant threat to the supply lines of the British Army, a fact not lost on the enemy who set about building up Bruges to the level of an Imperial Dockyard to harbour 30 destroyers and 35 submarines, and enormous resources were given to building heavy submarine shelters with supporting aerodromes.

The British answer to these threats took several forms, one of which was a force of 15-inch gun monitors, which, working with the spotting planes of the Dunkirk squadrons, bombarded the lock gates of the three harbours, without, however, bottling up the German flotillas. At the same time the operations of my father's squadron, No.5 Naval, were directed to bombing the ports, first by night, and later with the more powerful DH4 day bomber.

In July, 1917, Sir Douglas Haig asked for the help of the Dunkirk naval squadrons to support the offensive he was planning, which had the objective of capturing Bruges and the German submarine bases in Flanders, as well as turning the enemy flank. This major strategic plan called for a break-out from the Ypres Salient which would thrust behind the German right. The battles which followed were known as the Third Battle of Ypres and eventually bogged down in the mud of Passchendaele. 5 Naval Squadron's part in this battle was to bomb railway centres and airfields in order to draw enemy air strength away from the battle zone. These operations were interrupted when the Germans began the long-range bombing of London by Gotha night bombers, the first use of strategic bombing of population centres. There were immediate demands for elaborate home air defences to be created, and for attacks on the Gothas' bases near Ghent, my father's squadron being given the task.

The collapse of Russia in October, 1917, releasing large numbers of divisions from the Eastern Front, suggested that the enemy would mount a major effort in the Spring, to crush the Allies before the Americans arrived in strength. The point of attack was not known but the enemy's aerodromes were bombed regularly to hinder his reconnaissance work, 5 Naval moving south for this purpose, to the area of the old Somme battlefield. In a sense this was fortunate, enabling the squadron to play an important part in the desperate crisis of the March, 1918, Ludendorff Offensive, when it found itself at the point where a gap opened up between the collapsing British Fifth Army and the French, a crisis in which the Allies very nearly lost the war.

In the course of these operations my father flew on 101 bombing raids, all in the space of eighteen months – at this time of the war a pilot's life was reckoned in weeks. Tribute is also owed to the gunlayers. On their skill in lining up over the target and, perhaps at the same time repulsing attacking fighters, depended success or failure, and should the pilot be severely wounded, their lot would not be enviable. For both, flying in open cockpits at 16,000 feet or so without either heat or oxygen, there was an inevitable toll, yet, as this record shows, there was the pure joy of flying, the exuberance of a young man let loose in the air.

Nick Bartlett, 1993

1

Learning to Fly

I suppose I always had an ambition to fly, at least ever since seeing Blériot land in his small monoplane in a field near Margate in the summer of 1912; and occasional visits to Farnborough where my brother-in-law, Graham Weir, did his flying training in 1914-15 before being commissioned in the RFC whetted my appetite still further. On the outbreak of war in August, 1914, I was unfortunately unfit and when, a few months later, I applied to the Admiralty for a commission in the RNAS, although satisfying them as to my suitability, I was rejected on medical grounds due to some slight heart defect. I was at the time living in Kent and, thinking the medical standards for the Army might be lower, I presented myself to the local recruiting office with a view to enlistment, only to be told I would do very well in civil life but was no good to the Army. Very dejectedly I resumed my sedentary occupation, determined to try again later in the hope that reduced standards would enable me to overcome the medicos. The fact that two years later I took an aircraft up to 23,000 feet without oxygen, in an open cockpit, speaks for itself. In 1915 it was no fun for an apparently fit young man to be in mufti, and I well remember going to a garden party and overhearing two ladies making very disparaging remarks about myself – I am sure if white feathers had been available, I should have got one. However, towards the end of 1915 I applied again to the Admiralty and to my great joy was passed fit and told to await my call-up. That didn't come through until mid-March, 1916, and in the meantime I was in a fever of anxiety that the war would be over before I had a chance to get into it – I needn't have worried!

In due course I received instructions to report to the White City on 3 April, 1916, for a short drill and disciplinary course and, together with about a dozen other probationary Flight Sub-Lieutenants, spent a week drilling in the 'Court of Honour' of the old Franco-British Exhibition which by that time was looking a bit dilapidated but still possessed its pseudo-Indian turrets and arches which had blazed with thousands of lights in 1909. After a week of drill, lectures on 'traditions of the Service' etc, we reported to the RNAS station at Chingford for flying training. Flying training in 1916 was a fairly simple business when compared with present-day requirements. Training aircraft with a top speed of around 50 knots and capable of being landed at 40; a dashboard that carried only compass, air speed indicator, altimeter, side-slip bubble and, if the engine was water-cooled, perhaps a temperature gauge — as compared with the innumerable dials and complicated instruments of modern trainers. Any advantage of simplicity was, from the pilot's point of view, outweighed by unreliability and engine failures were frequent.

Chingford, in certain respects, was not an ideal beginner's aerodrome. Innumerable streams traversed it and were boarded over with wooden sleepers — it is now the William Girling Reservoir! The hangars backed onto the main Chingford-Ponders End road, immediately beyond which was a large and deep reservoir extending northwards for rather more than two miles. If the wind was from the north, which fortunately was not often, and one was lucky enough to clear the hangars and road on take-off, there was always the chance that a spluttering engine would land one in the 'drink' — the old rotary Gnome and Le Rhone engines were very prone to choke. There being no sleeping accommodation for trainee pilots at the aerodrome, we were billeted at various private houses in Chingford, a mile and a half away, and collected by lorry, usually at the unearthly hour of 5am in order to take advantage of still air. Those slow early trainers certainly, felt the bumps and any wind greater than about Force 2 was considered unsuitable for *ab initio* training. If the weather conditions proved unsuitable, we generally spent our time around the Gun Room piano loudly singing songs from *The Bing Boys* and other London musicals — *If you were the only girl in the world, She'd a hole in her stocking* especially come to mind, and there were others less mentionable. Actual flying training was interspersed with lectures on the theory of flight, aerodynamics, aero engines, navigation, meteorology etc, but I can't remember that we engaged in much sport or physical exercise apart from an occasional route march. Ben Travers, later to become famous as the author of *Rookery Nook* etc, gave us occasional 'pep' talks.

Ab initio training was carried out on Maurice Farman 'Longhorns' (MF7) and Graham White Box-Kites. I considered myself fortunate to be allotted to the MF 'Longhorn" powered by a 70hp Renault engine fitted behind the pilot and passenger nacelle; a pusher aircraft with a very wide elevator mounted on outriggers well ahead of the planes. I see from my log book that I went solo after 3¾ hours dual instruction, which was about average, and I well remember the feeling when my instructor on landing, climbed out and told me to "carry on". Once off the ground however, I felt quite confident. There was a feeling of lightness and buoyancy and after a few circuits and a fair landing I continued and made several more landings to my satisfaction. A few days later I suffered an engine cut-out at 500 feet, fortunately within range of the aerodrome, and after taking a few twigs off the tops of two high elm trees, landed safely in the middle of the aerodrome, much to the relief of my instructor.

Shortly after, I was promoted to the Avro 504K, powered by a French 80hp Gnome rotary, a slightly more difficult aircraft to fly on account of the torque due to the weight of a revolving engine which gave it a tendency to swing on take-off and needed a certain amount of correction in the air — all very easy once one was used to it. The Gnome engine also was very prone to choke if the mixture control was not correctly adjusted and valves were liable to stick up, especially on the Monosoupape variety. Rumour got around that this would cause a fire, and resulted in a certain amount of quite unnecessary 'wind up' and a tendency to cut one's engine at once if it gave a pronounced cough or bang. It happened with me once and I forcelanded in a small field with minor damage — the only accident I had during my training. A few hours on Avros and one graduated to the BE2c which was the most advanced trainer we had at Chingford. A nice aircraft to fly, powered by a 70hp Renault, its only vice was a tendency to tail-spin and though I never suffered one, others did with unpleasant consequences and a premature end to their flying careers. I took my 'ticket' after 8½ hours' flying time and on 17 August, 1916, proceeded to the RNAS Gunnery School, Eastchurch, for a fortnight's training on the Lewis gun and dummy bomb-dropping practice.

A local paper at this time reported, "A large aeroplane described many circles over Hawkhurst this morning and as the sun was shining brilliantly it formed a very pretty spectacle, and was witnessed by a great many people. We have reason to believe that the pilot was Lt C.P.O. Bartlett of the Royal Naval Flying Corps, who a few months ago was resident amongst us."

My chief recollections of Eastchurch are of a hilarious and very noisy crowd of trainee officers, rather more bawdy songs indulged in round the Mess piano and flying mostly on Curtiss aircraft from the very small aerodrome at nearby Leysdown on the Isle of Sheppey. John Alcock, later Sir John after his first crossing of the Atlantic with Arthur Whitten Brown in 1919, was the star turn at Leysdown. On coming in to land he would invariably cut his engine at about 2,000 feet, hold up the nose of his aircraft until the propeller stopped and glide in with such perfect judgement that he always ran on to the tarmac and almost into the hangar with a completely dead engine. Another stunt pilot of those days was Chris Draper who used to fly his Bristol 'Bullet' under the main line railway bridges and vertical bank between the hangars. A great fellow, Chris, who one met again later in France where he took over command of 8 Naval from Squadron Commander, now Air Vice-Marshal, Sir Geoffrey Bromet. Many will have read his entertaining book, *The Mad Major*, and will remember his trouble with the authorities after flying under most of the Thames bridges.

After completing the course at Eastchurch and successfully negotiating the passing-out examination, taken at Cranwell which had only recently opened, I reported on 1 September, 1916, to the RNAS station, Dover, then commanded by Squadron Commander Geoffrey Bromet, for a month's final training before proceeding to France on active service. The RNAS station was on top of the hill, near the Duke of York's School, and literally on the lip of the deep valley in which lay the town of Dover. I think it was Pemberton Billing who christened it 'The Valley of Death' as a large cemetery lay conveniently at the bottom of the hill, ready to receive a take-off crash, and the usual take-off was in a south-westerly direction immediately over the valley! The RFC aerodrome, Swingate Downs, was on the other side of the Dover-Deal road towards the South Foreland in a considerably less nerve-wracking area from the inexperienced pilot's point of view. Here, as at Chingford, we were billeted in the town and transport collected and returned us daily. The only new types I flew at Dover were the Bristol Scout, a handy little aircraft with an 80hp Le Rhone engine, and the 110hp Clerget Nieuport, both rotaries. One engaged in longer cross-country flights and I remember spending an afternoon at Manston looking up old friends, little thinking that years later I would spend six years there as station adjutant.

I had two forced landings while at Dover, one due to a broken petrol pipe on an Avro when I just made the aerodrome; the other on a Nieuport, the engine cutting dead when some distance from home and I just staggered over the perimeter hedge and sat down heavily — result, nothing worse than a bent axle, but I very nearly sat on top of the hedge.

One name that I can't pass over when writing of Dover is Flight Lieutenant Jullerot, a French pilot of very early vintage. My chief recollection of his flying, which he didn't often indulge in, is of flat turns; edging his craft round without any perceptible bank, doubtless as a result of the very early types on which he learned to fly. I'm not sure exactly what his official status was at Dover; he signed our log books, however. I think I am right in saying that he introduced the German wolf hound, now known as Alsatian, into England and that Wing Captain Lambe (later Air Vice-Marshal, Sir Charles Lovelock Lambe), who was in command of the Dunkirk squadrons, was the first

Englishman to possess one. A few days before I was due to leave for France, my father and mother came down to say farewell, and I remember how very kind the CO was when they came up to the aerodrome, calming, I am sure, any anxieties they may have had and giving them a rough idea of the locality in which I should be operating. Before proceeding abroad I had, of course, to kit up with khaki and Sam Browne, discarding naval blue which was still retained for ceremonial occasions and for going on home leave.

On 28 September, 1916, after breakfasting with my parents at the Burlington Hotel and completing my packing, I left Dover pier at 12.30pm in an ancient destroyer, *D55*, for Dunkirk, taking with me De Quincey's dog, addressed to Squadron Commander Haskins of No 1 Wing. An observer, Sub-Lieutenant England, RNVR, crossed with me. Shortly after leaving the weather came up pretty thick and we developed a corkscrew roll, the only casualty, however, was the poor old dog who had several attacks of mal-de-mer and seemed pretty sorry for himself, though he perked up wonderfully on sighting land – Gravelines church and the sand dunes. We drew into Dunkirk at 2.30pm alongside a destroyer moored against the monitor *Marshal Soult*, which two boats we had to cross to reach the quay. On the latter I saw the spot where a 20lb bomb had scored a direct hit a few days previously, killing and severely injuring several ratings. The deck plates were buckled and the huge armoured turret of her 15in guns splashed by flying splinters.

After waiting a few minutes a 5 Wing car arrived and I was soon speeding along to my new station at Coudekerque, some two miles inland, passing the cathedral, the west aisle of which had been more or less obliterated by a 15in shell (the Leugenboom gun, of which more anon). Arrived at Coudekerque, I soon recognized some familiar faces – Flight Sub-Lieutenants Parsons, Soar, Rouse and Chadwick, and after a brief interview with 5 Wing RNAS commanding officer, Squadron Commander Spenser Grey, sat down to a badly needed tea in the officers' mess, having had nothing since breakfast. So opened my career with 5 Squadron RNAS in embryo, for the squadron, eventually to become 205 on the formation of the RAF on 1 April, 1918, did not form officially until 31 December, 1916.

2

Introduction to Flanders

Before getting down to a description of 5 Wing RNAS as I first knew it in September, 1916, it would be well to recount briefly its pre-history from the time in August, 1915, when Wing Commander C. L. Lambe was appointed as adviser on aeronautical matters to Admiral Sir R. H. S. Bacon, who was in command of the Dover Patrol. This appointment gave Wing Commander Lambe control of the Dover–Dunkirk group of air bases which, at that time, consisted of 2 Wing under Wing Commander E. L. Gerrard at Dunkirk, which shortly afterwards was withdrawn and sent to the Dardanelles; and 1 Wing which replaced it on the St Pol aerodrome, Dunkirk and provided protective air and reconnaissance patrols for Admiral Bacon's long range bombardments, by monitors, of the German bases and installations at Ostend and Zeebrugge. In November, 1915, Wing Commander Lambe suggested that it should be possible for the Dunkirk Command to undertake a wider offensive policy in the spring of 1916, and he sought approval for the organization of a special bombing force by the creation of two additional offensive Wings and the immediate construction of new aerodromes in the Dunkirk area. He further suggested that 4 Wing at Eastchurch, consisting of four squadrons of six pilots each, should be transferred to one of the new aerodromes, and that the other Wing (5) should be made up by detaching four squadrons of six pilots each from 1 Wing at Dunkirk. These suggestions were approved and work on sites at Coudekerque and Petite Synthe was put in hand.

At the beginning of March, 1916, 5 Wing RNAS formed at Dover under the command of Squadron Commander Spenser D. A. Grey, from personnel of 1 Wing serving at Dover and Dunkirk, and began to take up its quarters at Coudekerque and, until fully equipped, came under the administration of 1 Wing. On 20 March, 1916, 5 Wing carried out its first operational mission when, in conjunction with French and Belgian formations, eight British bombers and four fighters carried out a combined Allied raid on the German aerodrome at Houttave and the seaplane base at Zeebrugge. Its equipment at that time, apart from one Flight of Sopwith 1½ Strutter two-seaters, consisted of French Breguet and twin-engined Caudron bombers. At its start, 5 Wing, Coudekerque, comprised A and B Squadrons and remained as such until 31 December, 1916, when they became 4 and 5 Squadrons, RNAS. The history of 5 Squadron, as such, may therefore be said to start from 31 December, 1916.

To get down to my own experiences on arrival at 5 Wing in September, 1916, perhaps I should start off by explaining that being a naval Wing, we adopted naval terms. We saluted the 'quarter deck', attended 'divisions' on Sundays, slept in 'cabins' and frequented the 'Ward Room' or 'Gun Room'; went 'ashore' in the 'liberty boat' ie into Dunkirk in a Crossley Tender. The 'lower deck' was given 'make and mends', the Master at Arms detailed 'port and starboard watches' — and so on. It all worked very well, we were an extremely happy station and right through all ranks there was a natural and unforced *esprit de corps* of a high standard. Let me try to recall the names of some of the officers of 5 Wing in the autumn of 1916. In command, Sqn Cdr Spenser D. A. Grey; F/Cdrs B. L. Huskisson and E. T. Newton Clare; F/Lts Coleman and J. C. P. Wood; F/S/Lts C. D. Booker, George Thom, Gerry Hervey, D. A. H. Nelles, R. R. Soar, T. F. Le Mesurier, Arnold Chadwick, G. M. T. Rouse, C. D. Sproatt, I. N. C. Clarke, A. M. Shook, Gardener, Moir and myself, St. John (Observer officer) Fowler (Intelligence) and several others. How the names and faces come back to me, and even their initials, but many were killed before the end of the first war and many others have now passed on; though a few still survive, mostly in Canada. [This was written in 1973.] They were a grand crowd and so were the 'lower deck'. Very few of us, I'm sure, ever wanted a posting back to 'Home Service' — life was far too eventful and friendships too firmly cemented. In the RFC I believe (I may be wrong), pilots were normally returned to Home Service after six months or so of active service flying, but in the RNAS one stayed out as long as one could stick it and could persuade the MO (Medical Officer) one was fit to carry on. I was myself in France for just over eighteen months before the MOs finally got their way; and that was immediately after the RAF came into being on 1 April, 1918, and former RFC medicos were sent to check up on former naval squadrons.

All RNAS units in the Dunkirk area came under the command of Wing Captain C. L. Lambe and were at the time, as far as I can remember; 1 Wing at St Pol aerodrome under Squadron Commander K. F. Haskins; 4 Wing at Petite Synthe under Squadron Commander Courtney; 5 Wing at Coudekerque; seaplanes based on *HMS Riviera* in Dunkirk harbour and the Depot adjoining St Pol. Later, several more squadrons were either formed at or transferred to the Dunkirk command — 2 (Photographic), 3 and 10 (Fighters), 7 and 7A, later 14, (Handley

Page bombers). My diary now comes to my aid and I think the best way to give a factual and clear picture of life and happenings in 5 Wing, and later 5 Squadron, will be to follow the diary day by day, skipping much that is of no particular interest, but retaining nevertheless a good deal in connection with station and Mess life and not confining myself merely to flying and operational happenings.

29 September, 1916

My morning spent looking round the station and familiarizing myself with its geography. The aerodrome is a good-sized field with plough on either side, farm buildings to the west and a narrow canal bordering the Dunkirk — Bergues road on the east. The northern end (Dunkirk) terminates in a fairly deep stream, lined by willow trees, all the hangars, living quarters etc being at the south end. Our aircraft (not detailed in the diary for obvious reasons) consist of two ageing Caudrons powered by twin 100hp Anzani radial engines, still quite serviceable for night bombing; about six two-seater Nieuports (130hp Clerget rotaries) and some dozen Sopwith 1½ Strutters (130hp Clerget). These last-named are our latest aircraft used at present for day and night bombing, the back seat being removed and the recess being fitted with a honeycomb bomb rack taking twelve French Le Pecq liquid 20lb bombs.

In the afternoon Reg Soar had to deliver a 1½ Strutter to the Depot and took me as passenger, doing a diversion along the coast to La Panne, halfway to Nieuport and the 'Lines'. Nieuport's piers and the flooded Yser down towards Dixmude clearly visible. We did several stall turns on the way back and a tight spiral down from 4,000 feet. He put his air brakes on at about 1,500 feet and couldn't get them off again and, as he was under-shooting and required his engine, he was in a bit of a flap! However, the tail didn't drop off despite excessive vibration and we made the small aerodrome all right. A car soon arrived from No 5 to collect us. (Reg did good work later, winning his DSC with 'Naval 8' on the Somme.)

30 September

Chadwick and I went into Dunkirk after lunch, had tea and caught the 6.15 car out to No 4 at Petite Synthe, where we dined. Their guest night and a great many old friends of Chingford and Eastchurch days. Chad was full-out on the piano and we had a rollicking time. Their wine steward, Macalone, was formerly chief cocktail mixer at Ciro's and we sampled a number. Left at midnight with a well-oiled seaplane merchant and had great difficulty in avoiding his pressing invitation to come aboard the 'Riviera' and have another drink! Arrived back at 12.30 am.

1 October

Sunday Divisions at 9.30. Rouse and Soar on patrol. At 5.10 I attempted to take up Nieuport 8527. The tail wouldn't come up and I started swinging badly; switched off and returned for a second attempt but the same thing happened though I kicked on full opposite rudder, held on to it too late, undercarriage collapsed and came heavily on to nose, breaking prop and burying engine some 3 ft. in the ground. Was thoroughly disheartened and cannot make out what was the matter having never had any trouble with Nieuports at Dover. Decided 8527 has a devil. (Two months later it did its best to kill me, but I killed it instead!)

2 October

I'm Duty Officer. Nothing much doing but the arrival of the Fleet Pay in the afternoon and payment of officers and hands provided plenty of work. Weather very bad and no flying in the afternoon, but Collett, Wood, Clark and Chadwick carried out an early morning raid on the Zeppelin sheds at Antwerp. Collett straddled the sheds, but Clark and Wood returned with engine trouble. Chadwick failed to return and there is no news of him.

5 October

Impossible weather for last three days. Still no news of Chadwick. In the afternoon I went into Dunkirk with Rouse and there joined Soar, Nelles and Orchard and caught our car from Jean Bart Square to Malo where the matron of the Queen Alexandra Hospital had arranged a sort of air service tea for our benefit. Several others there and a delightful tea, waited on by numbers of charming nurses in an enormous kitchen. Several songs were rendered by members of the staff, after which we explored the hospital with the nurses, including their dug-out which was pitch dark, so lots of fun.

6 & 7 October

Weather still impossible with hurricanes of wind and rain. We rigged up a Badminton court in an unused Bessoneau hangar and a number of us played including the CO and Huskisson.

8 October

Weather improved somewhat so our early patrols got away, but by 8.30 it was bad again and steadily got worse. After tea went for a 15-minute trip in a Sopwith bomber (1½ Strutter), a very fine machine with remarkable climb.

9 – 15 October

Bad weather continued, torrents of rain alternating with very strong winds. Rouse and I got down to work on our cabin, papering and redecorating walls and ceiling and putting up shelves. We secured a good rug in Dunkirk, also a porcelain basin from a shipbreaking yard which we fitted into a mahogany stand. With dark chocolate-brown wallpaper, curtains fixed, embroidered shelves and cushions and our photos and pictures on the wall, it begins to look quite like home, and instead of camp beds we have bunks.

16 October

Le Mesurier took up a 1½ Strutter for altitude test, but, his petrol propeller pump freezing, he couldn't get above 17,000. AA were very busy around Dixmude in the afternoon, the sky being full of shrapnel puffs.

17 October

I was Patrol Duty Officer, so up at 5.15 am. Weather unsuitable for early patrol but improved later and Soar and Booker took off at 8.30. I took up our only BE.2c and later Nieuport 8710 (not the one with the 'devil') and got on all right. These two-seater Nieuports have next to no glide; one just points the nose at the aerodrome and comes straight down. I came in too fast, didn't flatten enough, bounced and very nearly tipped over onto the nose at speed, but just saved it by heaving stick back hard – very near thing, the prop actually touching the grass. Took it up again in the afternoon and patrolled the lines from Nieuport along the floods towards Dixmude, but couldn't pick up Ypres as it was very hazy. Guest night and large number turned up from No1 and Seaplane squadrons.

This was the Nieuport 12c fighter of which 169 were used by the RNAS, and with the single-seater versions was one of the most successful and attractive aircraft of the War. During the critical period in 1915 when the Fokker Monoplane ruled supreme over the Western Front, Nieuports only could match them.

In a desperate attempt to halt the German advance in 1914 the Belgians had flooded the valley of the Yser. These floods which my father so often mentions formed the left flank of the Allied armies and provided the most miserable trench conditions on the whole of the Western Front.

18 & 19 October

Weather thoroughly bad again; will it never clear and let us get on with the job?

20 October

At last fine sunny morning with sharp frost. I was Patrol DO and got the first patrols away at 6.30 am. Orchard on Nieuport 8713 had engine trouble at 500 ft, just failed to make the 'drome and turned a complete somersault in the plough. Machine a write-off but he escaped with a few scratches and bruises. I took up Nieuport 8710 in the morning and practised stunts, lost engine on way down but made the aerodrome all right.

21 – 24 October

Nothing eventful beyond Thom landing Nieuport 8728 on the beach through engine failure, and Le Mesurier crashing the BE2c on taking off after balloon strafing. Guest night to do honours to those about to depart to the Somme, including Travers, Galbraith and Trapp.

23 October

I took up Nieuport 8710 in the morning. Very bad take off, swinging to the right. Johnson arrived in Sopwith Pup at 3.45 and did some hair-raising stunts near the ground – very bad form on a strange aerodrome and he was told off by the CO. Eventually he started off just as Soar was coming in on a Nieuport. The mechanic held onto his tail, and was lifted off his feet, lying along the fuselage, but managed to stop him after nearly careering into the ditch.

26 October

At 3.25 pm Wood, Hervey, Booker, Parsons, Soar and Thom left on 1½ Strutters for the Somme to form Naval 8 Squadron at Vert Galand. ['Naval Eight' was a crack fighter squadron and Booker achieved nearly forty victories.] News came through in the evening that only two of ours had arrived; two more were located and the other two missing. All eventually reached their destination, some after wandering across the Lines near Loos. Lt Hare, RFC landed on a single seater FE8 Monsoupape pusher which bore marks of shell-fire and scrapping. A nice fellow whom we were glad to have with us for several days of bad weather. Naval action in the Channel. Our losses 2 destroyers and an empty transport. Germans lose 2 destroyers.

28 – 30 October

Jope-Slade arrived from Dover. All patrols washed out for the time being.

Jope-Slade was my father's best friend until he was killed in a flying accident in Iraq during WW2. He produced 5 Squadron's magazine *DOPE* which ran to one issue and had poetic talent. On the subject of going home for leave roughly every four months, officers caught one or other of two ancient destroyers, *Greyhound* and *Racehorse*, and were generally encumbered with much kit and weighty souvenirs, such as 18lb and even 4.5in shells. Petty Officer Pitts was the Squadron's transport driver and evidently highly skilled.

If you're going on leave to Blighty
And you've left things rather late,
If the scheduled time for starting
Is a quarter after eight,
If you've only got five minutes
And you've hundredweights of gear,
By the beards of all the prophets
Pray that PO Pitts is near.

I know young men in civil life
Who think that they can drive,
Who've staggered round a racing track
And still remained alive,
But for sheer hair-raising driving
Let me recommend you PO Pitts.

1 November
Up at 6.45 for parade. Much better weather and Hare at last got away on his FE8. Sorry to lose him. I took up Nieuport 8711, one of the pair of single-seaters delivered from the Depot and known as the 'Hansom Cab'. A great improvement on the two-seaters and I climbed to 13,000 ft, the first 10,000 in 27 minutes. In the afternoon Collett, Saint, Woods and I practised formation flying. Gardner brought over the Breguet — a very large bus with a 250 hp Rolls-Royce engine.

This was the Breguet 5, a two-seater pusher as issued to No 3 Wing RNAS, for night bombing.

3 November
I flew the Sopwith 1½ Strutter for the first time — great machine. News of Chadwick in the *Daily Sketch*. He had been compelled to land through engine failure in a field near Tirlemont and couldn't set fire to his machine as he had no matches. He was helped away by peasants who lent him a peasant's cap and blouse and succeeded in hiding him for

several weeks in a chateau nearby. Eventually he was smuggled over the Dutch frontier. Hope he will soon be with us again.

The Sopwith 1½ Strutter was named from its W-arrangement of inboard struts. It was the archtype of the classic two-seater scout, and while being neither fast nor light on its controls, large numbers were built, including 4,200 by the French. It was introduced in 1916 primarily as an RNAS aircraft, with the 110 HP Clerget rotary engine.

6 November

Clear weather. Collett, Woods, Le Mesurier and Rouse formation flying in the morning. Orchard and Shook practising on Sopwiths. In the afternoon Rouse, Orchard and I formation flying on Nieuports. Good position keeping, too good at times especially over Bergues when I had to dive to avoid colliding with Rouse. It would have been my brother's birthday had he not been killed near Kut in Mesopotamia last April.

9 November

Preparations for a big raid as soon as the weather lets up. I am allotted Sopwith 9385 and tested engine ready for a start before dawn, as it promises a fine day tomorrow.

10 November

Up at 3.30 am. Not feeling too good after a bad night of violent indigestion, but I was certainly not going to miss the raid. Hot cocoa around the Mess stove. Le Mesurier, Saint, Nelles and Sproatt left on Caudrons at 4.30 am. I was the second Sopwith away, at 4.45 am. Ten more Sopwiths and one Nieuport followed. Bright moonlight but clouds coming up. Passed over Dunkirk and followed along the coast for our objective, the docks at Ostend. Into clouds somewhere off La Panne. Very thick and steered a compass course for some time, but mistrusting my compass came through the clouds at 3,000ft to find I was well inland, and the next thing I recognized was Dunkirk! By this time the red glow of sunrise was appearing in the east as a backcloth to bursts of HE above the clouds, but it was too late to make back; so I climbed to 14,800 feet awaiting sufficient daylight to land with bombload. Sunrise above the clouds was a glorious sight, the moon at the same time shining brilliantly. Very cold at 15,000 in an open cockpit with no protection other than Sidcot suit, helmet and gauntlets. Landed at 6.32 am. Sproatt and Blagrove also failed to reach target, and Jope returned with his bombs which failed to release. The Doc told me I should not have gone up and knocked me off the midday stunt, which, however, did not come off. Turned in early feeling pretty rotten and not much better next day.

12 November

Sunday. After breakfast Allan Perrett and Bailey arrived on Baby Nieuports to escort our bombers. We all left, eighteen of us at midday. I was first away on Nieuport 9205. Entered clouds at 500 feet and emerged above them at 1,500 and circled until several others appeared. Some six of us then headed for Ostend. Clouds were a wonderful sight, a sea of snow with very occasional gaps. Passed over Furnes and headed out to sea. Clear of clouds for a short while, but heading NE for our objective were soon over them again and solid with no gaps anywhere, but brilliantly sunny at our height. Continued for ten minutes climbing steadily, then noticed aircraft ahead circle for a minute and head for home. A thin streak of bright brown smoke fell past close by my port wing, which I realised must be the trail of a 20lb Le Pecq bomb. I decided to come lower and look for a possible gap in the clouds. Down to 3,000 feet and circled for some time. Eventually through a tiny gap spotted I was over land, so headed north and at once saw bursts of HE ahead of me. Made for them and pulled off my bombs when I judged I was over Ostend harbour. No other aircraft in sight so headed west by south and climbed to 10,000 feet. Nothing visible but clouds and after steering due west for some 25 minutes, caught a glimpse of flooded land on my port. Studying this I gathered I was making very little progress, evidently against a strong west wind, and so continued for another fifteen minutes to be sure of not coming down in enemy territory. Shutting off, I struck the clouds at 2,000 feet and was still in thick clouds at 400 feet. At last saw fields dimly very close below, opened up at once and fortunately the engine responded. Could see nothing at over 200 feet and at that height only a very short distance. Headed north for coast flying for some twenty minutes at 100-200 feet. Passed over a fair-sized town which for a moment I thought was Bergues, but soon decided otherwise. Continued north-west and, at last, the coast. Decided I had overshot Dunkirk and so turned east by north, but looking at my watch discovered I had been in the air two hours and ten minutes, and my fuel only being sufficient for 2¼ hours, decided not to risk a forced landing from 200 feet over strange country and, spotting a good-looking field, brought off a good landing just in time, with petrol almost gone and lubricating tank empty.

Several French soldiers quickly on the scene and relieved to find I was 'Anglais'. Found I was a mile from the village of Oye, six miles west of Gravelines. Secured a temporary French guard while I made off for a telephone. After about an hour I succeeded in getting through to the CO, who seemed greatly relieved to hear I was OK and sent a car forthwith. An excellent French soldier who spoke quite good English was a great help, arranged for the guarding of the 'bus and escorted me to Oye, where the car picked me up at 5.30 pm, after interviewing the senior French officer and relieving his guards with our own. Back at 7 pm and reported to the CO.

Everybody seemed to have had the same trouble as myself, some worse. Collett and Orchard got as far west as Calais, but, flying Sopwiths, had sufficient fuel to get back. Woods also came past Gravelines; Le Mesurier came down in the sea and suffered cuts and bruises, but his Sopwith floated and after fifteen minutes he was picked up by a destroyer; Moir landed at Hondschoote and Jope, on coming through the clouds found himself at 200 feet over the German front-line trenches and was blazed at with machine guns and rifles. So, much to the discomfort of old man 'Gerry', dropped all his bombs on them and shot back into the clouds. He eventually came down at Furnes aerodrome and crashed but was unhurt. His machine was holed in many places. Three planes landed at St Pol and a No 1 Squadron pilot came down in the sea off Calais. Everyone had an eventful time and we were indeed lucky to have no serious casualties. Only three pilots actually caught sight of Ostend. Newton–Clare came down to about 100 feet over the town and saw a cyclist fall off his bicycle in alarm. Mallet of Seaplanes was killed on a Schneider Cup★ which folded up in the air. Ostend again tomorrow before dawn if weather suitable. Altogether an eventful Sunday. Guns very heavy in the evening.

13 November

Thick mist early but began to clear by 11 am and I left in the touring car with petrol and oil and a mechanic for Oye. Engine started up at first swing and I made a good getaway between two trees. An EA was bombing No 4 shortly before I passed over their aerodrome but no damage. Allan landed on a Nieuport from No 4 with McLaren as passenger at 9.30. Thick clouds at 1,500 feet so no Ostend stunt.

★ Sopwith Schneider single-seat floatplane.

3

Nieuports, Sopwiths and 'Flaming Onions'

Night bombing was pioneered by the French using Voisin pusher aircraft in 1915 and was taken up the following year by the RNAS flying Sopwith 1½ Strutters and a few older twin-Anzani-engined Caudron GIVs which carried an observer or bomb aimer as well as the pilot. The Sopwith's rear seat was removed to accommodate a honeycomb bomb rack taking twelve French 20lb Le Pecq liquid-anilite bombs. These required very careful handling and contained nitrogen peroxide and petrol which were mixed in flight by a propeller which opened two compartments. The explosive was manufactured during the bomb's fall and no detonator was required. [I well remember one of these bombs lying around the house during the 1930s.]

One took off down a paraffin flare path usually about two hours before dawn and on the return journey hung around until the light was sufficient to see the ground clearly enough for landing. Our usual night targets were the docks and shipping at Ostend, the submarine docks and pens at Bruges, and the Mole and shipping alongside at Zeebrugge. All three were heavily defended by AA and rocket batteries and bristled with searchlights, while more searchlights were spaced along the coast right up to the Dutch frontier, especially at Westende, Middlekirk, Wenduyne and Blankenberghe.

A truly wonderful fireworks display attended us on our night stunts, the long chains of vivid jade-green balls which streaked up, invariably reaching one's height before falling away and dying out, were a magnificent sight providing they didn't come too near. They must have been in the nature of a range-finder as they always seemed to come to, or slightly above one's level, at whatever height, before fading out, and were immediately followed by HE bursts pretty well on target. We called them 'Flaming Onions' and at first imagined that they were connected by a wire which would entangle one's propeller; but of course they were not, their regular spacing, like a glorious jade-green necklace being due to some sort of machine mortar from which they were fired. I never heard of their doing any damage but occasionally one fell on a wing, being quickly swept off by the slipstream, the fabric only showing a slight scorching, but I wouldn't have welcomed one in the cockpit.

The advantage of coastal targets was that one could creep up the coast two or three miles out to sea without being heard, then turn in when approximately level with the objective, so giving the defences very little warning of one's approach. If one was heard, the signal went up from Nieuport and was repeated all the way up the coast, on came the searchlights and the guns were ready for you.

15 November
A priceless early morning, clear with a half moon, so all up by 4 am. Caudrons away at 4.55 and I was fourth Sopwith off at 5.20. Followed up the coast a mile or two out to sea. Westende and Middlekerke batteries already at work and searchlights busy. Off Ostend at 8,000 at 5.50. AA blazing away and searchlights sweeping in every direction, also quantities of flaming onions. Shut off and planed down silently over the docks at 3,000, releasing my twelve bombs as far as I could judge straddling the Atelier de la Marin, but was unable to observe the bursts and was in the thick of rockets and AA bursts for the next few minutes, one of the former uncomfortably close. Headed out to sea climbing hard and circled a mile or so off the piers for about ten minutes watching the display as other machines came over the target, but it was beginning to get light and Ostend, its channels and basins were clearly visible, so I made for home. Westende and Middlekerke still in action as I passed. All aircraft returned safely, though it was at first thought that one of No 4's big Shorts* had gone down in flames. Later, however, to our relief, this proved to be unfounded. Orchard missed Ostend — how, I can't think — and bombed Zeebrugge instead. This was the biggest raid to date so far as weight of bombs dropped goes, and it seems likely that heavy damage was inflicted. I observed one big blaze to the west of the docks. Altogether a priceless stunt which I thoroughly enjoyed.

After lunch Jope and I walked into Bergues, a highly interesting old town, cathedral with fine stained glass. Moats and old fortifications surround the town which contains some picturesque old buildings, notably the Bellfroi and the ancient abbey of St Wino. A good eight miles walk there and back which should help to keep us in trim. Norman Glaisby arrived from Dover — good to have one of the old White City crowd out here.

16 November
I was squadron D.O. Very cold indeed. Norman took Nieuport 8711

---

* Short bomber landplane

up after lunch for a look round. He made a bad landing, bouncing some 12 feet but only bent the axle.

17 November

Off Ostend at 6.5 am at 11,000ft. Shut off and planed down towards the town from the N.E. Saw many bombs exploding on and around the Ateliers de la Marin. Searchlights and AA busy and many green chain rockets coming up. Came over target at 6.10 at 5,000ft and loosed off twelve Le Pecqs and was immediately picked up by searchlights, several of which coned me, for dive, turn and dodge as I would, I could not shake them off. Several guns were quickly on to me and the air seemed full of bursting shells and green rockets. From the noise of the explosions and brilliance of the flashes they had my range pretty accurately. With full engine I pushed the old Sopwith down to 110 knots and streaked out to sea, soon shaking off those infernal searchlights. Well out to sea, I again circled for several minutes watching the fun as later arrivals came over – a great sight and vivid red flashes from our bombs around the docks area. All aircraft safely back by 7.20 am. There were eight degrees of frost on the ground and it was mighty cold up top. Daily Admiralty reports in the press under such headings as 'Hornets nests raided' etc.

21 November

Better weather after three days of rain and wind but no raid orders. Sproatt and Slade did their first flights on Nieuports, the latter crashing on landing and turning completely over without, however, much damage apart from the prop and none to himself. I was going up for mirror practice on a Sop, but owing to a cracked propellor only one machine was available. Collet and I tossed up and he won but was soon down as clouds were at 900ft.

22 November

Orchard, Rouse, Saint and myself down for a raid but washed out by the weather. At 2.20 four Sopwiths left for a raid on Zeebrugge, escorted by two Sopwith and two Nieuport fighters. I was on Nieuport 9205. Followed the coast past Ostend and Blankenberghe and patrolled between the latter and Zeebrugge at 11,000ft, observing many bombs burst around the Mole, one hitting a vessel moored on the inner side from which a huge column of black smoke rose. Plenty of AA, nothing very close though I felt a couple of hefty bumps from bursts below me. Aircraft over the target got a pretty warm reception but no enemy planes sighted. Jope and I went into town by the 6 pm car, meeting Jones and Trayner and returned with them to No 1 for dinner.

26 November
Allen from No 4 did some great stunts on a baby Nieuport; a half loop and sideways roll-over (lacing the shoe). A very nice rabbit-skin chest and back protector arrived from home.

27 November
It is being said that raiding is being washed out for a month apparently on account of jealousy and ignorance on the part of an old-fashioned Vice Admiral, who doesn't like to see the RNAS doing better work than his monitors can accomplish.

28 November
All our single-seater Nieuports are being replaced by two-seaters – worse luck. At 2.5 pm I escorted our bombers on Nieuport 8728 with gunlayer Milne in the back seat, for a raid on Zeebrugge. AA slight and bad visibility prevented observation of results. On the way back I went down to investigate a large aircraft below which turned out to be a Voisin. We landed just in time as fifteen minutes later a heavy ground fog obscured everything. Frames of A Squadron, Furnes, was killed landing in the fog, hitting a tree.

29 November-4 December
Hard frosts and heavy mist and fog has grounded us for days on end. I took over the Mess wine accounts from Shook.

5 December
Very windy and stormy. Rouse, Norman, Orchard, Jope and I went into Calais in the Crossley tender, picking up Shaw from No 4. Lunched at the Hotel des Sauvages and spent the afternoon shopping, finishing up in a cinema. Returned at 5.30 pm. Corbett killed yesterday on the Somme when flying with Naval 8.

7 December
Very misty but cleared a little after lunch when Alexander came over from No 1 and nearly crashed his Nieuport on landing. I took Sopwiths N5082 and 9385 up for test. Very good concert given by Lena Ashwell's concert party at Malo Casino at 5.30 pm; big crowd from all Wings there. Afterwards dined at Tavern Charles, alongside the blitzed cathedral, with Alexander, Vernon, Gow, Casey and Munro.

11 December

After two days of rain and strong winds, at last a fine crisp morning, though glass very low. A day of crashes. Orchard did in a Nieuport as a result of a very bad landing. He nearly wrote himself off and a hangar on coming in far too fast, at the last moment opening out his engine and skimming over the top, finally crashing the undercarriage on his second attempt. Collett, with Moir as passenger, choked his engine on taking off from the Depot on a 1½ Strutter, attempted to turn at 150 feet, stalled and nose-dived into the ground. Collett was very lucky to escape with a broken ankle and bruises, Moir being badly shaken and battered about the head and legs — a light let-off for both. A French Nieuport crashed in the sea, and a Voisin and a seaplane crashed into the docks. Trapp of No 8 killed on the Somme.

13 December

Le Mesurier took up the 130hp Clerget Sopwith for test — 10,000 feet in fifteen minutes. I took up Nieuport 8741 with Gunlayer Duggan as passenger. Engine very weak at take-off and I only just cleared the hedge. Clouds at 1,500 and visibility bad, so came down low and zoomed along the beach past La Panne and back at 50-100 feet. Slade and I shot sparrows round about the farm and fields after lunch.

16 December

Fine, though hazy morning. Le Mesurier, Nelles, Glaisby and I left with flying kit for the Depot at 10.15 to fly Nieuports across to Dover. Got away at 11.30 and circled over Dunkirk at 2-3,000. I was on 8527, my *bête noir*, which I crashed on first arrival at No 5. We set out in formation for Calais to cross from there. Visibility very bad and thick scudd coming up fast at 4,000 from the west. This and a dud engine decided our leader, Le Mesurier, to turn back, those being his orders if conditions at all bad. So, on the 'washout' signal we turned back. Glaisby, however, lost the formation and proceeded on his own, eventually reaching Capel and finally Dover. Sickening — I would certainly have crossed if I had been on my own, especially had I known how 8527 was to let me down later. Hope to get across tomorrow.

17 December

Raining hard so little prospect of crossing. At 2.40 pm news came through that conditions were all right at Dover, so hustled into our kit and prepared to leave. Visibility here very poor and masses of threatening clouds rolling up from the north-west. First machine away at 3.10 and others took off and circled at 1,000 feet, getting formation, when orders came through to 'washout'. Shook, however, missed the signal and made straight across on his own and, after flying all the way in thick cloud at 6,000, luckily struck Dover all right but with very little daylight to spare. Heavy rainstorm here at 4 pm.

20 December

Thick fog for the last two days and another false start. Today overcast early but clearing by 11.30. All eight of us in our Nieuports by 12.20. I should have been first away but 8527 would not give her revs. After many attempts Potts (engineer CPO) managed to work her up to 1130, but she was not steady and required full petrol. I was not at all satisfied but on his advice and being anxious to get away, all the others having already taken off, I decided to chance it. Result − engine cut out just as I was taking off and, in consequence, I ran into the plough and old 8527 stood gracefully on her nose. Little damage beyond a broken prop but sufficient to prevent my getting away today and the weather conditions are ideal. Saint returned with rev counter adrift, having choked his engine. The other six got across but Hewson crashed badly on the Dover RFC aerodrome. Le Mesurier arrived back with a new 1½ Strutter at 4 pm, and Gardener returned on a Sopwith Triplane.

22 December

I went up with Le Mesurier in twin-engined Caudron. From the front seat one has a very clear unobstructed view, also no windscreen so a very fine blow. 'Mezzi' did a spiral and two steep nose dives over Dunkirk (110 knots). A fairly strong wind and face felt mighty cold with no protection in front.

23 December

Weather hopeless for the last two days and today a terrific gale blowing. Nieuport 8527's trouble diagnosed as an airlock in the petrol tank − vent completely corroded up. Hewson's crash occasioned on taking off from RFC aerodrome, his engine failing when just over the hangars, and he attempted a turn and nose-dived into the ground. Machine a write-off and he is badly cut about the face and knee.

The French seaplane base went up in flames. We secured a car and went down to the monitors from which we had a good view. Base completely gutted and most of their 150hp FBAs★ destroyed.

★ Franco-British Aviation flying boats

24 December

Sunday and Xmas Eve. Attended 9.30 Service in one of the hangars and, immediately after, Saint and I proceeded to get our Nieuports ready to cross to Dover. What trick, I wondered, would old 8527 play on me this time — perhaps drop me in the 'drink' halfway across? At 11.30 we climbed aboard. To my disgust it was discovered that my propeller was loose and it was 12.30 before that was put right, Saint having pushed off alone in the meantime. Engine revs nearly 1200, so she should be OK. Took off, engine pulling well until, at 400 feet, she cut dead over the outskirts of Dunkirk! No landing possible ahead, so turned back for the aerodrome dropping fast. As I had taken off into a brisk wind, I dared not attempt a down-wind landing, especially as many of our Sopwiths were lined up in front of the hangars. At 60 feet I attempted to turn into wind but with no engine and insufficient height, couldn't get her round, and from 40 feet she fell out of my hands. Fortunately, insufficient height for her to get her nose down and she hit on port wing and engine, more or less disintegrating, all four longerons breaking just behind my back. Well, I thought, as I sat in the shambles, that's the end of you old girl — you've done your best to kill me, now you're dead and can trouble me no more! Found I was all in one piece and nothing worse than a hefty bump on the forehead and a black eye. By this time dear old Norman Glaisby and Jope, who had witnessed my take-off and return, were running across the aerodrome to extricate my mangled remains, and were surprised to see me step out of the debris. They wanted to support me off the field and wouldn't believe me when I said I felt perfectly all right and as steady as when I went up. Head began to buzz later and I am in for a lovely black eye! Coleman arrived from Dover on a 1½ and Newton-Clare on a Triplane. Two crashes at St Pol, so it's been a crash Xmas Eve — and a Sunday.

25 December

Xmas Day. I made my crash and a bit of a head an excuse to lie in all morning and so missed Wing Captain Lambe's inspection. We had our Xmas dinner at 6.30 — a very fine spread and wine ad lib. (The menu, autographed by all present, still reposes in my diary — signatures all clear, though some in pencil.) An uproarious evening culminating in a great soda water syphon strafe. Jope got the CO full in the back of the neck at close quarters and we all got more or less drenched. Norman won 400 francs at roulette. Kept things going till 12.30 am when Polly, Fellows, Norman, Jope and I walked down as far as the water works for an airing. Turned in at 1 am. Sproatt and Rouse return from leave tomorrow and I go the next day.

28 December

Hard frost early. I left aboard the *Greyhound* at 9.30, but low water delayed us for an hour and there was further delay owing to a minefield laid by the Huns last night, which our minesweepers were busy clearing. Atkinson of No 4 and an RNVR Sub-Lieutenant crossed with me. We were not invited down below for an hour and a half and it was perishingly cold on deck. At last we thawed out in the Ward Room, but it was cramped and stuffy and when the old *Greyhound* started corkscrewing halfway across, we preferred fresh air on deck. At last the white cliffs of Dover loomed ahead and we made the harbour at 1.30. After collecting the garrison pass, caught the 3.30 to town and rolled in at the Stanhope Hotel at 7 pm; next day travelling down to my home in Gloucestershire. I went down with 'flu and colds for much of my holiday, doubtless due to the old *Greyhound*, but I managed to get in some golf and other activities.

4

Bombing U-Boats by Night

13 January, 1917

For some reason no destroyer running, so, after lunching at the Burlington with De Quincey, Edwards and Hamilton, we chartered a car to Folkestone and boarded the transport *Onward*, an old SE boat, and at 3.30 left together with another transport, accompanied by three destroyers. A comfortable and quick passage and a great improvement on the *Greyhound*. Arrived at Calais 5 pm but no car to meet us. However, Edwards succeeded in getting through to No 1 who promised a car forthwith, but after dining at the Grand we had to wait till 9 pm when two cars arrived, one from HQ and the other from No 1. Both had been held up in a snow blizzard.

14 January

Snow and rain most of the day. Nothing much seems to have happened since I went on leave. Le Mesurier, Clarke, Gardener and Shook have got their second 'ring' also Thom and Booker on the Somme with Naval 8.

15 January

A hard frost and sunny morning, but conditions not so good at 2.30 when I took A. M. Bamforth as passenger in Sopwith N5102. Difficulty with the engine and did not take off till nearly 3 pm when conditions had deteriorated greatly. Into the clouds at 400 feet but through them at about 1,200 and gloriously sunny over a sea of cotton wool, but not a gap anywhere, so, not wishing to get lost, the visibility below being very bad indeed, I reluctantly left the sunshine after a few minutes and came down through the murk to find myself luckily 300 feet above Coudekerque. Visibility by this time was extremely bad and I had three or four attempts to get in, as snow and ice patches combined with weather conditions made it impossible to judge the perimeter until almost at ground level. However, I contrived a fair landing at last. The extremely cold and bad weather continued for several days so that we were largely confined to the Gun Room, where Saint, Rouse and Glaisby were busy with their model aircraft factory, building Triplanes and 1½

Strutters, while I wired and made a new propeller for my Etrich. The only other relief was one very full-out evening resulting in the demise of Mess property, mainly chairs and glasses. Jope (now 'Dope' on account of his editorship of 5 Wing's magazine *Dope*, first edition just produced) was in great form and exceedingly witty and amusing.

22 January

Still extremely cold and frosty. Walked into Dunkirk in the afternoon and met Rigby and Lusby in the patisserie for tea. Wood was there and afterwards met Winter and Dingwall and a number from No 1 and we all repaired to the Tavern Charles to refresh. Got back to find Chadwick had returned and we read his fascinating account of his adventures in German-occupied territory near Tirlemont. The Belgians had rendered him immense assistance at grave risk to themselves. He spent several weeks in a large chateau in charge of some of the servants of its departed owner, which was frequently searched by the Germans, but fortunately one of the rooms possessed a secret cupboard and though they tapped the walls they never tapped low enough to discover it. He was smuggled across the Dutch frontier one night with eighteen others, the German sentry being bribed £25 a head.

23 January

Awoke to intense cold, water bottle, sponge etc frozen stiff. Someone said their hot water froze as they poured it out − I don't think! Beautifully sunny, crisp morning and cloudless sky, but twelve degrees of frost even at midday. Formation flying in morning and afternoon.

24 January

Intense cold continues; 22 degrees of frost and from the air one sees frozen foam all along the beach and some distance out to sea. Formation flying morning and afternoon. I kept pretty close and several times got badly tossed about in other people's backwash. Engine missing considerably all the time and only running on one magneto. Did steep spirals over the Docks. Walked into Dunkirk with Jope and Thompson for tea. A big strafe going on all day long at the lines and heavy gunfire all night.

29 January

So cold this morning that water in basin covered with thick ice. Weather still crystal clear. Six of us left at 11.55 am for raid on hostile shipping. Followed the coast as far as Ostend but saw no sign of shipping in enemy waters. Extremely strong east wind so that on turning back we were off Dunkirk in an incredibly short time, so much so that I was almost bombing our own destroyers off Malo as we were over them within about five minutes of leaving Ostend. Bitterly cold at 12,000. The last day or two there has been heavy firing along the Lines, seemingly in the Dixmude area. Huns overhead at 10.30 pm. AA batteries opened up and a few bombs dropped somewhere in the town direction. Brilliant moonlight night and 23 degrees of frost at 11 pm.

2 February

Coldest night yet, 28 degrees of frost at 8 am. Everything frozen solid including the soda water syphons, paraffin in stoves and all the milk. Newton-Clare, Le Mesurier and Clarke left for England at 9 am to bring back Triplanes. Two inches of snow on the ground, possibly that is the reason we are not flying – a somewhat feeble one though the confines of the aerodrome might be a bit difficult to distinguish. I spoke too soon; there is to be a raid tonight. Our machines allocated and busy testing them. After tea I had to search Dunkirk to try to secure eight electric stoves to prevent oil and bombs freezing on our eight aircraft for tonight's raid, but couldn't raise even one! At 9 pm I heard Nelles was to take my machine, his own being out of action. Very disappointed after so many weeks of inaction. Heard No 4's Shorts and Caudrons pass overhead at 10 pm. Heavy cannonade in the night.

3 February

Eight of our aircraft left at 4.45 am but many of them came to grief, only Rouse and Nelles (my aircraft) reaching the objective, Bruges Docks. All the rest had engine trouble due to the castor oil freezing to a tallow consistency as a result of the intense cold – 40 degrees of frost! Sproatt and Chadwick landed at 5.30 am, engine revs having dropped below 900. Blagrove and Gardener landed on the beach and could not get assistance to haul their aircraft to safety from the incoming tide. Wood circled overhead for sometime waiting for dawn with a failing engine and eventually crashed badly on the bank of the stream at the north end of the aerodrome, snapping off two stout willow trees, crumpling his wings and reducing the fuselage around the pilot's seat more or less to matchwood, but miraculously he escaped with a few cuts and bruises and a sprained ankle. At 8.30 am I proceeded to the beach with six hands to help Seaplane's salvage team secure Gardener's machine which was floating in a nearly vertical position in eight feet of water. We had to wait some time for the salvage team to arrive with motor boat and tackle, then securing a rope on to the tail we towed her in till she grounded. With the assistance of 30 or 40 French soldiers we endeavoured to haul her in, but she was stuck fast with wheels embedded up to their axles and there was nothing for it but to wait till the tide receded and dig her out. Garrett arrived about 11 am to unbomb her and as the tide dropped we shovelled a passage through the frozen foam and surf on the beach, which was some three feet thick. At length we were able to dig the wheels partially clear and, with several lifting the tail and all hands on the rope, were able to haul her well above high water mark and, disarming her, Garrett and I proceeded home with bombs and guns, leaving the Depot to collect her remains. Quite ready for lunch and a warm-up, having been wading in frozen foam and slush all morning. The sea was covered with floating blocks of ice! Blagrove's Sopwith was towed into the seaplane base.

In the afternoon five enemy aircraft (EA) passed directly over No 5, dropping some small bombs without effect. With supreme contempt for the French AA, they flew at 3,000 feet and no shots went anywhere near them. There were six crashes today at No 4. A Short ran into the ditch in the dark and was then run into by another Short, and Sieveking crashed badly landing on the beach in a Caudron and is suffering from shock. Altogether a somewhat disastrous day and, to cap it all, returning from their raid last night, No 4's Shorts dropped a couple of 65lb bombs in our vicinity, which exploded with terrific force but causing no damage. In the evening the whole of our Somme contingent turned up for dinner – Huskisson, Hervey, Thom, Booker, Soar and O'Hagan, also Leslie. Festivities kept up well into the morning. Newton-Clare, Clarke and Le Mesurier returned from England with Pups and a Triplane.

6 February

After six inches of snow yesterday, awoke to the coldest morning I've ever experienced. Thermometer 10 below Zero F (42 degrees of frost). All the oil frozen in aircraft tanks, so Norman (Duty Officer) says. A clear and brilliant day. Brisk walk to keep warm after tea. The snowbound countryside looked most picturesque under the light of a full moon. EA over Bergues during and after dinner, many bombs dropped and Bergues batteries active, plenty of rockets and flares.

7 February

Another perfect morning and very cold. I was squadron DO. Eight Sopwiths left at 12.55 for a raid on Bruges, accompanied by Tapscott and Chase on a photographic machine from No 1. Saint returned early with loss of revs. All returned at 2.30 with the exception of Blagrove on fighter N5102, with Medgett as gunlayer, and no news of them by nightfall.

8 February
Still no news of Blagrove though Chase reports having seen his plane down low heading for Holland, so there seems little doubt he is interned there. Twenty degrees of frost again last night. Six of us left at 12.15 for raid on hostile shipping. I was on fighter N5222 with Gunlayer George behind. Followed coast up to Zeebrugge against a very strong east wind, it taking us 80 minutes to get there, ie a ground speed of 40mph. No shipping at all observed beyond Nieuport. Very clear and could see well into Holland; Zeebrugge harbour appeared to be ice-bound. Back to Dunkirk in about ten minutes. EA paid us a visit before dinner and later several were over Dunkirk and Bergues. Many large bombs dropped, AA very active but no searchlights.

9 February
Up at 7 am for parade. Over 30 degrees of frost in the night. Five EA came over just after 7 am, plainly visible at 10-12,000 feet. Many more bombs dropped on docks. Plenty of AA but mostly wide. Nine of us received orders to leave at 3.15 for a raid on Ghistelles aerodrome. I was on N5082, Le Mesurier and St John leading on N5096. On pumping up pressure I got a stream of petrol past my head and discovered the pipe to the gauge was broken. Impossible to get it righted in time and, to my disgust, I had to remain behind. All the others were away in 60 seconds and returned safely after a very warm reception, several being holed. Only five out of the nine reached the objective, Le Mesurier, Glaisby, Stewart and Chadwick returning with engine trouble. AA was exceedingly accurate and intense and it was impossible to shake off the gunners who kept their range accurately from the moment they approached the target at 15,000 feet till after they had crossed the Lines on the way home. Ghistelles is about ten miles inland from Ostend. Sorry to have missed that experience in daylight, but shall no doubt have plenty of opportunities in the future. Clarke had a jagged hole torn in his engine sideplate, just missing his left leg. No stunt tonight as engines can't be got ready in time. Wright joined us from No 1.

10 February
Tests and local flights only. I took up N5222 (Sopwith 1½ Strutter) for test after magneto overhauls. She is revving distinctly better but room for plenty of improvement. Got her up to 10,000 in 25 minutes which is as good as she will ever do with her present engine. Practised steep

stall turns and vertical spirals. Had a distant view of Ypres. Woods left for England, his nerves having gone all to pieces after a few weeks at the Somme.

11 February

Weather dud so projected stunt washed out. Sunday Divisions at 9.10. Only three degrees of frost and looks like snow with a falling glass. Griffin, recently arrived, went up for a practice flight on N5082 and Wright afterwards attempted one but broke his prop taking off. After lunch Thomson, Griffith and I walked into Bergues and explored the ancient walls and fortifications, turning in at the usual place for tea where we met four army officers and had an interesting and jolly chat round the fire.

12 February

Rouse and Sproatt left for England to collect Triplanes or Pups – lucky blighters, prospect of several days in town this weather.

13 February

Six of us left at 2.40 pm for a raid on hostile shipping. I was fighter escort with Smith as gunlayer. Patrolled coast as far as Blankenberghe without sighting anything. Very clear view of the Lines and observed much activity. Off Ostend two Pups dived into our formation and we all swung round to make sure of their identity as the Germans have a very similar aircraft up the coast now. Glaisby blazed away at one which dived straight at him, doubtless to the surprise and discomfort of its pilot.

14 February

Up at 3.20 am for a raid on Bruges. I was off at 4.40 am on N5093. Followed coast past Ostend and turned in over Wenduyne. Very dark and hazy night and difficult to pick up the coast line. Planed down silently to 3,000 over the docks and loosed off, seeing my last bomb explode near their western end, so as I dropped on a line north-east to south-west, the others must have straddled the target. Searchlights picked me up low down and I heard a couple of HE bursts fairly close, but I dived and zoomed out of the glare only to be picked up again by another. Soon shook that off and, engine picking up well, climbed hard for the coast. Uneventful return. 15,000 feet off Dunkirk waiting for daylight. All back safely except Stewart and had no news of him till after lunch. Having failed to pick up the coast he got completely lost, eventually attempting a down-wind landing in the dark in a ploughed field with disastrous results, but luckily escaping injury. He found himself near Oost Capelle, seven or eight miles south-east of Bergues. EA paid us two visits at midday and at 5.15 pm. Nelles and Le Mesurier went up at midday but saw nothing of them. In the evening a Triplane and six Nieuports from No 4 gave chase, also two French Voisin 'Cannons' but didn't make contact. One man killed and sixteen seriously injured at the Depot and several aircraft destroyed. Berlin reported "...great damage at St Pol aerodrome, hits and conflagrations."

16 February

A raid planned for yesterday called off on account of the weather. Today up at 4 am. A clear and starlit night but only a slip of moon left. Took off at 5.15 am for Bruges. Very dark and had to keep a sharp lookout for landmarks. Off Ostend at 5.35. A few searchlights and rockets soaring up. Carried on past Blankenberghe and turned in over Zeebrugge following the canal down to Bruges. Shut off and glided down to 1,800 feet over the target which was lower than I had intended or cared for, but I didn't want to switch on and give my position away. I could see the docks, and clearly, as it was beginning to get light. Just before releasing my bombs there was a huge red flare-up almost immediately below me which seemed to fully illuminate my machine and I felt sure I would be seen at such a low altitude. However, though I heard a few shells explode there was nothing uncomfortably near and searchlights never picked me up. On opening up my engine, however, I at first only got a few splutters as the plugs must have oiled up on my long glide down, and I was down to 3-400 feet only before she began to pick up, gradually working up her revs as I headed up the canal for the coast. I could see Blankenberghe and Ostend quite clearly as I passed them in the grey light of dawn. On arriving off Nieuport I turned down along the Lines and followed them past Dixmude to Ypres where, shutting off, I circled down to 2,000 feet, having a good look at the battered remains of the place. The salient showed up well. Landed at 7.15 am. Le Mesurier chased an EA which had been bombing Dunkirk but, his gun jamming, he had to break off. Two eulogistic reports from the Admiralty on our recent raids.

23 February

After several days of rain and fog it is thick again today and nothing doing, so Jope, Rouse, Chad, Griffin and I left at midday for a trip to La Panne and Nieuport. A good lunch at La Panne and continued to Coxyde and Nieuport, leaving the car in what is left of the Cathedral Square. Explored the town which is practically levelled. The Cathedral, which must have been a fine and large one, is a mass of fallen masonry, and the Hotel de Ville the same. The whole place is a shambles tenanted only by a few French soldiers. While we were exploring, a battery of French 75s opened up nearby and as counterfire started we felt discretion the better part of valour and returned to the car.

24 February

A bit clearer. Ward broke his prop when taking off, the mud being so appalling and splashing up yards high, and both the other machines stuck fast on landing with mud up to their axles.

25 February

Weather still very thick. After lunch, together with Wood, Rouse, Le Mesurier, Warwick Wright and others, visited the monitor, *Sir John Moore*, where the First Lieutenant showed us round explaining and illustrating the working of her 12-inch turrets; taking us into the magazine and, for our edification, elevating and depressing the guns and revolving the turret. Depth of turret between 40 and 50 ft. Had tea in their snug Wardroom and returned by 5 pm.

> The monitors of the Dover Command were slow ships of about 7,000 tons with huge anti-submarine bulges, mounting two 12- or 15-inch guns. They had performed good service in 1914 supporting the Belgian army in the desperate Battle of the Yser, and in 1917 made several attempts to destroy the lock gates at Zeebrugge and Ostend, which they damaged, as well as sinking two submarines and a floating dock. To avoid the heavy coast batteries they had to fire at a range of 26,000 yards.

26 February

At last a fine and breezy morning which should soon dry up the surface of the aerodrome, the mud and slush yesterday causing a split prop. Newton-Clare had a bad crash on N5114 with Warwick Wright as passenger. He choked his engine taking off and hit a large tree lining the Dunkirk-Bergues road, snapping it in half. Both suffered severe bruising and were lucky to escape with nothing worse.

1 March

It seems we may be saddled with the French 109th Bomber squadron (Voisins)*, though how on earth we are going to fit in twelve of those

* Large pusher biplane with 47mm Hotchkiss canon for ground attack.

large aircraft plus their complement of officers and men, heaven knows; especially as the first Handley Page squadron is due to form at Coudekerque shortly. A French pilot landed a 'Cannon' Voisin this morning to test the suitability of our aerodrome and, unfortunately, was quite satisfied. Wing Captain Lambe brought some officers of the 109th over in the afternoon. Our first Handley Page should have arrived from Manston but turned back on encountering fog and clouds off the French coast. Three of No 1 Squadron's aircraft were attacked by five Halberstadts*. Edwards, with Chase as observer, was wounded in the shoulder and both feet, but Chase managed to shoot down their attacker. Edwards succeeded in landing all right and was rushed off to hospital.

2 March

Had a good look at the new 130hp Camel with two synchronised Vickers guns — some machine; can make rings round a Triplane.

4 March

The first Handley Page arrived from Manston at 3.30 pm, piloted by our CO, Spenser Grey, with St John, Barker, Polly and a gunlayer as passengers. Weight 3½ tons empty, fully fuelled five tons. Capacity 400 gallons, endurance 10hrs, powered by two 250hp Rolls Eagle VI engines. Armament three Lewis guns and 14x112lb bombs. Speed 75 knots. Later models are to be fitted with 300hp Sunbeams. A colossal machine.

9 March

After four days of bad weather, today is slightly better. Shook and Jope flew the Sopwith Pup. I was to take her up as soon as she had been filled up but this taking longer than had been expected, I went up with Barker in the Handley Page, Wood and Griffin also coming. I found the front turret extremely draughty and cold but wonderful for observation. We flew over Jean Bart Square at about 1,000 feet, apparently causing much excitement from the large number of people gazing up at our vast bulk! Quite a novel sensation right up forward with nothing but a low parapet round so that one can hang well over the side and look sheer down. [This was Handley Page 0/100 bomber No 3116.] Chris Draper and eleven of his pilots arrived from Luxeuil to be temporarily accommodated here until there is room for them at No 4. Frightful scrum, six of them sleeping in the Gunroom.

* Halberstadt D2. Precursor to the Albatros. More respected by Allied pilots than its own.

11 March

Better weather at last. I took the Pup up after lunch, one cylinder cutting immediately after take-off; nevertheless she climbed well and I was able to do some steep banks and stall turns. Extremely sensitive on controls, spirals nicely and has an amazing glide. Good landing but so very sensitive fore and aft that she is apt to hunt if not handled very lightly.

> In spite of its low horsepower but dependable Le Rhone engine, the highly manoeuvrable Sopwith Pup had the edge over all enemy fighters during parts of 1916-17, being able to 'hold its height' in a dogfight. It was remembered with affection as the perfect flying machine by both RNAS and RFC pilots, and was the first plane ever to be landed on a ship, by Sqdn. Cdr E. H. Dunning in 1917. Top speed was 101 mph at 10,000 ft.

13-14 March

Several of the Luxeuil crowd departed. Jope and Norman are temporarily transferred to No 1 Squadron together with two gunlayers for spotting. They are not enthusiastic! After a talk with Huskisson it was definitely decided that I should throw in my lot with 5 Squadron (bombers) as I had not been awfully fit from time to time. Though sorry to miss the opportunity to fly Pups, Camels and Triplanes, I have never regretted joining No 5.

15 March

Feeling very rotten so cut breakfast and stayed in bed, lunching only on milk. Weather improving so took up N5222 (1½ Strutter) for 55 minutes with Barker as passenger. Did some verticals, several steep spirals and stalls, so much so that poor old Barker felt quite ill in the back seat. He would sit backwards and watch the tail most of the time, which he said vibrated like mad on steep turns and quite put the wind up him! After tea I took our wine steward, Smith, up for 40 minutes. It was his first time in the air and he seemed to enjoy it. Some fine cumulus clouds. Chadwick, Moir and Le Mesurier flew the Pup.

16 March

Overcast and clouds very low. I took up N5093 for engine test after lunch, Barker as passenger. Speed test along the sands between Dunkirk and La Panne, 100 knots at 20 to 50ft. Later flew up the coast to Calais and back, and, it being much clearer in that took her up to 9,000ft. Engine thoroughly satisfactory. Nichol, instructor on the BE2c during my sojourn at Chingford and now a Flight Commander, came over to tea from No 9 Squadron. Jope, Glaisby and myself are officially transferred to No 5 Squadron. A revolution in Russia and abdication of the Czar.

17 March

Fine clear morning and Huns dropped a large bomb near Malo hospital wounding three. At last the Triplane people have returned, flying over from Dover. Jope and Glaisby returned from No 1 squadron.

21 March

Gales of wind for the last three days and now it is snowing, Moir, Gardener and Le Mesurier fetched Pups from the Depot. Little landed, or rather got down, on a Triplane at 4.30, tearing off a tyre and narrowly avoided crashing. He left again for Furnes at 5.30. [R. A. Little DSO, DSC, was credited with a final score of 47 victories, and was killed in action in 1918.]

22 March

Snow in the night and early morning. Later formation flying, but precious little formation about it. Stewart broke his prop taking off and flew for half an hour with the whole of the leading edge of one blade missing!

24 March

Huns paid us a very vigorous visit this evening. A large number of heavy bombs dropped in the Dunkirk-Malo direction and much machine gunning. AA and searchlights active but as usual they failed to pick up a single aircraft. Plenty of shell splinters whistling down. The largest raid on Dunkirk since I've been here.

25 March

Sunday. Oliver was killed on a Triplane. He was seen to enter a cloud whilst on a bank at about 2,000 feet and a moment later reappeared side-slipping badly; the large single strut apparently collapsed under the strain and the machine went onto its back. Both sets of planes were wrenched off and the fuselage came down whistling like a bomb.

Only 150 Sopwith Triplanes were built. It was very much an RNAS fighter and, with its tremendous rate of climb, became the terror of the enemy for a short while. Raymond Collishaw's flight of five Triplanes of Naval 10 destroyed 87 aircraft in May and June, 1917. However, it was soon supplanted by the more heavily armed Camel.

28 March

I've been laid up for the last few days with a howling cold and tummy trouble, but better this morning. Formation flying at 2.30 pm. I accompanied Jope on 9896. Conditions pretty dud, very hazy and cloud layer at 2,000. After 30 minutes we flew over to Bergues and explored the old town from a very low altitude.

29 March

Rough and wet morning. Most of us visited No 4 Wing at Petite Synthe preparatory to moving there within the next few days. Afterwards went on to Fort Mardycke to see the position of the buoy on which we were to carry out live bombing practice.

30 March

Rough and stormy so no live bombing practice. 'Mournful Mary' the siren on top of Dunkirk cathedral tower, awoke the echoes at 8.45 pm and the firework display began a few minutes later. Numbers of EA over between then and midnight and, from the sound of their engines and rattle of their machine guns, they were at no great height. A large number of bombs, including a few heavies, dropped over Dunkirk, but little damage of consequence.

1 April

Busy packing for our move to Petite Synthe. Disposed of the fittings of our cabin to Sieveking for 60 francs. No 7 Squadron (Handley Pages) will soon be installed here.

2 April

We prepare to decamp to Petite Synthe and No 4 to Bray Dunes, consequently the quarter deck looks as if a whole suburb was moving house. Le Mesurier, Clarke, Gardener and Nelles ferried four aircraft across at 9 am, but weather then became too bad to take the remainder.

No 4 Squadron left before lunch with the exception of Chadwick. The remainder of us left at 6 pm in various cars and tenders. Jope and I have secured Sieveking's cabin, but it will need a lot of structural alterations and re-decoration. Snow blizzard all the afternoon. A huge crowd for the Mess. No 11 Squadron, Canadians, were celebrating the departure of two of their members for the Somme and drinking champagne by the bucketful, consequently much noise and rough-housing and many windows and chairs broken. Newton-Clare, I think, was rather disgusted and rightly so; however No 11 are thinning out by degrees.

3 April
Blizzard in the night and, having left our window partially open, we awoke to a snowdrift, Jope's gramophone having to be dug out. Weather cleared by midday and three of the big Shorts left for Coudekerque after lunch. Clarke, Gardener, Nelles, Jope, Norman, Stewart and I left for Coudekerque to bring back 1½ Strutters. Two aircraft got away all right but Jope's prop split before he had got his tail off the ground, the mud being so bad, and it was decided not to risk any more, so we returned by transport having plundered much wood etc from our old cabins.

5

Testing The Latest Bomber

No 5 Squadron was by now more or less installed at Petite Synthe, where we were to remain for the next eleven months, at first under the command of Squadron Commander E. T. Newton Clare and later Squadron Commander S. J. Goble. Although the official date of the formation of 5 Squadron, RNAS, is recorded as 31 December, 1916, we always felt a more appropriate date would have been 1 April, 1917, when the two squadrons, Nos 4 and 5 (originally 'A' and 'B') parted — 4 to Bray Dunes and 5 to Petite Synthe. Moreover, whilst at Coudekerque the functions of the two squadrons were rather intermixed, pilots of either carrying out fighter patrols or escorts and sometimes bombing raids. I was never quite certain myself to which squadron I belonged, my log book week by week bearing the No 5 Wing stamp and being signed sometimes by Flight Commander Huskisson (fighters) and sometimes by Flight Commander Newton Clare (bombers), and recording about as many fighter patrols on Nieuports as bombing raids on 1½ Strutters. Another curious anomaly was that although referred to as squadrons, they were commanded by Flight Commanders and 5 Wing itself by a Squadron Commander. It all seemed a bit mixed! Once arrived at Petite Synthe, 5 was definitely and solely a bomber squadron, carrying out mainly night raiding while still equipped with 1½ Strutters and becoming a purely day bombing squadron on re-equipment with De Havilland 4s during May and June, 1917.

The good old 1½ Strutter was still in use in the squadron up till the end of July, 1917, though rarely for day-raiding purposes. It was a delightful aircraft for night flying, being so stable, and, having an adjustable empennage*, it was only necessary to set this for level flight and one could fly hands off ad lib in the quiet, bump-free conditions usually experienced at night.

5 April
A fine sunny morning. After two or three attempts to land Norman

---

* The rear part of an aircraft, comprising the fin, rudder and tailplane

came down at about 90 knots with brakes full on, touching in the middle of the drome and of course running full into the ditch which he hit at about 50 knots going 20ft up into the air and coming down on his nose in the plough. Fortunately only a buckled cowl and bent nose piece. At 1.15 pm ten of us left for a raid on St Michael Junction, south of Bruges. Conditions were very threatening and visibility almost nil, the washout signal being given in due course. I was the sixth down at 1.45 pm and the first to land with a whole prop, all the others splitting on take-off due to the appalling mud. In all, fifteen propellors have gone in the last three days! Sproatt arrived from England and Chris Draper gave a fine exhibition of stunting on a 130 hp Baby Nieuport. The anniversary of my brother's mortal wound at Telaya while leading his men (Siege of Kut).

6 April

Struggled out of bed into flying gear at 3 am. Seven of us left for St Michael Junction. I was on N5150 and a strong following wind brought me level with Ostend at only 5,000ft, my engine pulling very badly. Scores of searchlights as I turned in between Ostend and Blankenberghe, but though they flashed across me several times they failed to hold me and I planed down to 2,000ft in search of the junction. Visibility was bad and the ground very indistinct and I searched for twenty minutes before at last spotting what I thought to be the target and pulled off, but not a single bomb would release and, try as I did, I could not get them away and so had to return with a full load. It was getting light as I turned homeward and two heavy bursts just below me suggested that I was visible to the gunners, but they must have been haphazard shots, much to my relief. I made very slow progress against the strong wind, landing at 7.5 am. Don't like 5150. She suddenly dropped her right wing on landing and slithered to within a few feet of the ground. Everyone had great difficulty finding the target and some bombed Bruges docks instead.

7 April

A Flight holding themselves in readiness for a stunt under Army orders. B and C Flights left at 12.45 pm for a raid on Zeebrugge Mole, escorted by six Baby Nieuports*. All returned around 2.30. Jope had a cylinder

---

* The Nieuport 17 'Baby' was one of the most popular fighters of the War, being chosen by the top aces, Ball, Bishop, Guynemer and Nungesser. it was much used for 'balloon busting' when fitted with Le Prieur rockets, and many of its features were copied by German designers.

blown off by an HE burst over the target, but, thanks to a strong following wind, just made the aerodrome, the remains of the cylinder and piston falling into the cowl on landing and jamming the engine. He was actually able to use his engine a little at times, the con rod of the damaged cylinder being shorn through, but the vibration was terrific. All aircraft were heavily shelled. Our stunt (A Flight) is to bomb the docks at Ghent. We are due to leave at 3.30 am tomorrow.

8 April

Easter Day. Called at 3 am and started to hurry into our kit, but a few minutes later the raid was washed out on a bad weather report − back to bed, thankfully.

13 April

After five days of bad weather, snow and blizzards, it is at last clear with huge cumulus cloud formations. I took Le Mesurier up in N5150 for engine test. Very fine above the clouds. Landed at Bray Dunes and stayed for lunch, meeting many old friends. They have brought their cabins up to a wonderful standard of perfection. Thorne and Peters of Naval 8 killed on the Somme and Hewett missing. Le Mesurier took the reins on the way home through thick and threatening clouds. We went for a 5-mile tramp.

14 April

Called at 3 am for a raid on Zeebrugge. A shower and heavy clouds coming up from the west delayed our start for 1½ hours, so that we left in daylight at 5.30 am. I took N5504, a 65lb bomber belonging to C Flight and loosed off over the Mole at 6.15 am. Gunners evidently not expecting us as low clouds were partially obscuring the target, but they opened up as we were getting well out to sea. The big gun (9 in) batteries at Knocke had a knack of opening up on one when feeling safe well out to sea. A Triplane was recently hit at 22,000ft when off Zeebrugge. Visibility had become extremely good and I could see Westende firing at me on my way home, but being well out to sea there was nothing near. Very slow business coming back up wind. Landed at 7.30 am. Ormerod crashed on landing and Gardener and Wright landed at Bray Dunes and Furnes respectively with engine troubles.

15 April

Chris Draper's birthday which the Canadians celebrated very thoroughly as they set out to sample every one of the 49 drinks on the list! As previously mentioned, Macalone, our wine steward, had been chief cocktail mixer at Ciro's and what he didn't know about cocktails wasn't worth knowing. A riotous evening and Spenser Grey came over from Coudekerque and was shouldered despite violent struggles. Turned in at 1.30 am.

16 April

Cooke, Griffin and I left on the 10 am destroyer for the usual periodic leave. On the way through town I called in at the Air Department to enquire about flying an aircraft back on my return. Seems likely I shall get one.

24 April

After an excellent leave, on the instructions of the Air Department, I reported to Brooklands and took over Sopwith Pup A6176. Being unable to get a meal, I took off at 1.30 pm on an empty tummy. Delightful little aircraft and climbing splendidly but at 3,000ft the haze was so thick that I could not see the ground sufficiently to pick out landmarks. Set a course south-east but it got more soupy and at 1,000ft I could barely see the ground. However, I recognized Tunbridge Wells and from there flew on to Hawkhurst, feeling very squirmy as castor oil fumes were seeping into the cockpit, which was not helpful with an empty inside! I did several loops over Hawkhurst Moor where my friends, the Steads, quickly had a large Union Jack out on their lawn, having guessed who was visiting them. Came very low directly over the garden waving a welcome and zoomed up completing two more loops before setting course for Dover, where I landed being unable to stomach any more fumes from the engine. Tea and eggs put me in somewhat better condition while my Pup was overhauled. She was found to be in pretty poor condition, the flying wires being very slack and no end play in the aileron controls. Newman said it was a wonder I had got down all right and that she didn't fold up. Apparently Hawker★ stunted her abnormally when he put her through her tests at Brooklands. I saw Sproatt, Calder, Alexander, Jullerot and others, also Cooke and Griffin who had failed to get aboard the destroyer. An RFC pilot crashed in flames on the RFC aerodrome (Swingate Downs) and was killed. I left Dover at 5.50 pm and essayed more loops over the harbour, but for some unknown reason the engine cut momentarily each time I got on my back and I found myself suspended by my belt looking down from an inverted position on the shipping in the harbour until she side-slipped out and, getting her nose down, the engine picked up. These evolutions, accompanied by another 'gas' attack, decided me to push out to sea without further delay and I was soon over Cap Gris Nez and beating up against a strong wind along the coast. Clouds at 400ft over Dunkirk and very bumpy below. Landed at 6.55 pm at the Depot and handed over the castor oil-fumed Pup. Half a dozen other Luxeuil pilots landed just after me from Paris, and a car soon arrived from Petite Synthe to pick me up. I find there have been several raids since I left nine days ago. Nelles failed to return from a raid on the 22nd on St Denis Westrem. He was seen by Le Mesurier descending low over Holland but no news of him yet. Masson killed through a Baby Nieuport breaking up at 5,000ft coming out of a roll.

Nelles later wrote: 'You may be interested in the circumstances which resulted in my being interned in Holland. As was usual we flew well out to sea skirting the coast and turned in near the Dutch border, receiving some HE shelling near Zeebrugge with one or two bursts being dangerously close, but I was not aware of being hit. However, my air pressure dropped although the small wooden prop. on the air pump on the half strut was revolving, but without gasoline the engine stopped. I violently operated the auxiliary hand pump beside my seat, but without effect, so there was nothing to do but head for Holland where I landed well in a field, in course of being ploughed, near the town of Costburg. The farmer did not stop his ploughing for even an instant but I had him in mind to hold the tail down in the event of my re-starting the engine. Believing the air leak to be the result of a loose connection I was busily trying to locate it when I was surrounded by Dutch troops who climbed all over the plane and took me in charge.'

25 April

Early raid prevented by the weather, but later one got away for Zeebrugge and hostile shipping. I was Raid Officer and got five aircraft off in fifty seconds. Lambe was present. Four returned by 5 pm. Clarke was attacked by an enemy seaplane and had his engine put out of action by a bullet through the cam-box and his aileron controls shot away, but without any lateral control he landed safely on the sands at La Panne. Four Handley Pages went on a similar mission an hour earlier, three returning. The other, piloted by Hood, being shot down by a seaplane a few miles off Westende and landed on the sea where it was heavily shelled. Both petrol tanks were pierced. Two French flying boats made a gallant attempt at rescue but one was crippled by a shell. The other picked up the wounded gunlayer and

* Harry G. Hawker, the celebrated Sopwith test pilot.

got away. Finally an enemy patrol boat towed the damaged French aircraft into Ostend. No news of Hood and the third gunlayer.

27 April

Honours List received. Newton Clare awarded the DSO, also Huskisson, and three DSCs. We celebrated at a special dinner at Coudekerque — a very full out evening. The same afternoon five of us, led by Gardener, left for a raid on Zeebrugge. We circled for forty minutes off La Panne waiting for our Triplane escort which never turned up. The visibility had by that time become very bad with a thick cloud layer all over Belgium, and Gardener fired the signal to return. I was on Jope's bus and crashed it on landing through doing a steep turn about twenty feet up with bombs on.

29 April

I took up N5150 for test in the morning: climb with 250lb bomb load reasonably good but she needs truing up, and behaves very queerly near the ground. Sands landed a large Short on the CO's office at Coudekerque this morning, ripping off the roof and completely wrecking the machine. The CO was fortunately out.

1 May

Griffin, taking off for Zeebrugge, lost his engine fifty feet up, and side-slipped into a field on the other side of the railway. His machine completely crumpled up with pilot's seat and engine telescoped. Impossible to see how he escaped with only a cut face and was able to walk away with help.

2 May

Four of us left at 5.30 pm for a raid on Ostend docks and shipping escorted by Triplanes. Turned in over the town and docks at 11,000ft. On approaching I got a colossal burst immediately below which threw the old Sopwith fully fifty feet upwards, or so it seemed. On return Cooke said he saw me being shelled with bursts of HE above, below, and mostly behind me, but apart from that one below nothing worried me. Our fighters of 9 and 10 Squadrons plus the French ace, Nungesser, accounted for six EA today, a large photographic bus secured by Newbury and Hall at 18,500ft falling close to Coudekerque.

The French 'ace' Lt Charles Nungesser, was a brilliant pilot whose silver Nieuport scout had a roving commission over this part of the Front. He was credited with 45 victories and died in 1927 attempting a trans-Atlantic flight.

4 May

Very hot and hazy day. Machines all being teed-up for moonlight raids. One EA came over and dropped four tiny bombs at 10 pm. Tapscott had two of the half struts on his Sopwith cut through by HE over the Mole while on photo-reconnaissance today.

7 May

Called at 1.15 am for raid on Bruges. Eight of us left at 2.30 am, myself on N5150. Followed the coast past Ostend and turned in over Wenduyne. Beautifully clear moonlit night but ground mist made visibility difficult. Not a searchlight all the way until approaching the docks at 3,000ft they all suddenly sprang to life and for two or three minutes I must have been visible to the gunners against the moon which was behind me. I came in for an almighty strafing, the noise of bursting shells and their flashes on my planes were incessant, at times illuminating my cockpit. Equally alarming were the long green 'chains' of flaming onions streaking across my bows in all directions. The docks showed up clearly in the light of rockets and gun flashes. Dropping my bombs without delay I was glad to get clear of the enemy 'hate' at 3.25 am. Passing close to Blankenberghe I fired a dozen rounds or so into Ostend for good measure and then climbed hard, having an hour to wait for sufficient light to land. I managed to get old N5150 to just over 17,000 over Calais and continued as far as Cap Gris Nez. The rising sun gave me a marvellous view of the Kent coast from about Whitstable round as far as Folkestone, and of the French and Belgian coasts right up to the Dutch frontier and beyond. I noticed a tremendous strafe along the Lines in the Lille and Arras direction. Landed at 4.40 am. Ormerod on return crashed on the beach just our side of Nieuport piers, the wreckage of his plane being salvaged later in the day under shell fire by Gardener, Cooke and Garrett. Cleghorn on return followed a cloud bank which he took to be the coast and landed near Ashford! One way of getting home to Blighty, though some farm labourers took him for a German and approached with pitchforks. Le Mesurier brought over our first DH4 from Coudekerque.

9 May

Clarke, Dickson and I left at 10.45 am for a raid on hostile shipping and, finding several vessels off Ostend, bombed them, including a large one apparently anchored. Our bombs fell close but no actual hits obtained. I was on N5153, a 130hp Clerget 1½ Strutter, a lovely aircraft to fly with a fine engine. After lunch several of us went over to St Pol, meeting Norman, Tapscott, Hervey and others. We studied Nungesser's 130 h.p. Nieuport with his device of skull and crossbones, coffin and candlesticks enclosed in a large heart emblazoned on the side of his fuselage. Our Pups took off very quickly when the EA alarm was sounded. Shook and Smith of 4 Squadron (Bray Dunes) accounted for an Aviatik over Ghistelles and Enstone got another in the morning.

10 May
Fully expected to be called early this morning, but apparently too misty. Clarke brought over our second DH4 and nearly crashed on landing at his second attempt, coming in much too fast. Clarke, Dickson and I left at 3.15 for Zeebrugge Mole, picking up our escort of three Pups over La Panne. Visibility fair and AA heavy over the Mole, about a dozen bursts near, but a mile or two out from the coast thick haze prevented them seeing us. Moir, one of our escort, failed to return and no news of him.

11 May
Mist again prevented early flying. Busy getting DH4s bombed and ready. Gardener took up DH4, N5967 with McSorley after tea and put up a good performance on her. I took up N5150 for test at 6.55 pm, a new engine and a good one has made all the difference to her. Revs 1100 climbing. Some good cartwheels on the way down. Still no news of Moir.

13 May
Very hot and thick haze and clouded up after lunch. Standing by for a raid but washed out at 4.30 due to poor visibility. Later I took up N5221 with Jope in the back to test the TST bomb sight, but found it useless from the pilot's seat, requiring one's whole attention with one's head in the region of one's knees in order to scrutinize the ground glass screen, and impossible to keep the machine on a straight and level course.

14 May
Continuing very hot, close and overcast. Lieutenant Commander Sturdee and a naval surgeon came over to lunch with Page (Command Medical Officer) from Coudekerque. Newton Clare took Sturdee for a joyride on N5221, and I was to have taken the surgeon on his return, but valves and plugs needed attention and by the time this was done

rain had set in. Jope and I went into Dunkirk in Doc Page's car and met Sieveking, Tommy Norman, Stewart and others at the Arcades; Jope, Tommy, 'Pin' (Sieveking) and I going on to dine at the Rue du Bassins.

Report on the monitor's operations against Zeebrugge on the 12th seems highly satisfactory. Two of our spotting machines, Fowler and Gow and Tapscott and observer, at 14,000 a mile off the Mole protected by very numerous fighter escort, the monitors having their own aerial escort miles out to sea. Tapscott went down into Holland early, and Fowler and Gow carried on for four hours, only just reaching home with petrol exhausted. Many aerial combats in all of which we were successful.

15 May

Landing practice with our new DH4s. Jope landed all right at the second attempt, but Cooke had eight attempts, coming in much too fast and having to go round again until he at last got down safely. I took her up after tea and liked her, though she handled differently from the 1½ Strutter. After the experience of the others I tended to bring her in on the slow side, but put her down quite gently at the first attempt. (Petite Synthe was a considerably smaller aerodrome than Coudekerque, which was one of the reasons we had to give the latter up to the Handley Pages. In addition to being smaller it was much more restricted in its approaches. Lengthwise, east to west, it had reasonable length with a road at one end and open fields at the other, but across, north to south, it was a bare 350 yards and one had to approach over a main railway line bordered by our hangars and other buildings; while on the far side a large timber yard with stacked timber to a height of some twenty feet ran much of the length of the perimeter. Consequently with our DH4s we always endeavoured to take off lengthwise, even if this sometimes meant the hazard of a moderate cross-wind. – Author's Note).

16 May

Gardener brought over the first 200hp Hispano Sopwith bomber from the Depot after lunch for testing. Known as the B1, serial number N50, it had a reputed performance of 115 knots in level flight and a ceiling of 20,000 feet with a 440lb bomb load. All the old Coudekerque crowd came over to dinner in honour of the CO's birthday and the recent promotions and decorations – a full-out evening.

18 May

Gardener tested the Le Pecq bomb release gear on the Hispano Sopwith. I took up Sopwith N5221 for test in the morning with Cleghorn in the back. One cylinder kept cutting out due to a seized tappet. After lunch I took Paul Bewsher (an HP observer from Coudekerque) in 9375 to test the Udale carburettor. Extremely windy and gusty (Force 7) and almost out of control at times below 4,000ft. Above 6,000 it was steady though one almost stood still against the wind. I gave Bewsher a good look at the Lines. It was so clear one could see the houses in Ostend from Furnes. Landed at Coudekerque and had tea, meeting among others Brackley and Lance Sieveking, known as 'Long Pin' on account of his altitude compared with his brother Victor, who was himself of no mean height. (Lance was the well-known producer of plays in later life.)

19 May

I took St John back to Coudekerque after lunch in Sopwith N5081, the best 1½ I've ever flown. Stunts beautifully and doesn't tend to get her nose down even in a vertical spiral. An RE8 from Bailleul landed at Coudekerque and took off just after I arrived. Its attempt at a zoom was really comical. After holding her down for 200 yards or more we thought something spectacular was coming, but the wretched thing only staggered up some 50–100ft. I flew back with Fellows, just returned from sick leave, in the back seat.

> The RE.8 was the most widely used British two-seater on the Western Front. Its great stability was at the cost of manoeuvrability and it suffered great execution by the nimble Albatros.

20 May

Our three DH4s and the Hispano Sopwith left at noon for a raid on hostile shipping. All returned at 2 pm after attacking destroyers off Zeebrugge. After lunch Gardener told me I could take up the Hispano Sopwith for a trial flight and that I was to fly her while he was on leave – thrilled! I took her up for 35 minutes after tea. Thick clouds at 6,000ft. She has an amazing climb – the first 1,000ft in 30 seconds – and is fast on the level, zooming 600ft from level. Easy to handle but very heavy on lateral control, and fairly streaks away from a 1½ Strutter.

> The Hispano-engined Sopwith B1 single-seat bomber N.50 was the only one of its type. Designed as a long-range high altitude aircraft, speed was 110mph at 10,000ft with nine 50lb bombs aboard. It was later used to develop a 2-seater reconnaissance machine, the Grain Griffin PV.N50, with folding wings, of which seven were built. These were the prototype

of the carrier-borne torpedo bomber which was to play so large a part in the Second World War.

21 May

Bennett and Mather reported missing, and Buster Gaskell and Malone killed on the Somme. Standing by all day for a raid on St Denis Westrem aerodrome, but weather didn't let up.

25 May

After four days of bad weather we were called at 3.15 am for a raid on St Denis Westrem aerodrome. Le Mesurier with St John, Jope, and Cooke with gunlayers on the DH4s and myself on the Hispano Sopwith left at 4.15 am. Followed the coast up to the Scheldt, passing just west of Flushing and then turned south-east for Ghent. Very good visibility and from Ghent could see Antwerp, Bruges, Brussels and the flooded Yser. I made observations from 14,000ft over Gontrode airship station and then descended to 6,000 and loosed off over the hangars and buildings of St Denis Westrem, seeing several hits among the hangars and three in the château grounds (officers' quarters). Turning, I dropped the remaining ten bombs on a second run over the target and these Darley (Jope's gunlayer) observed to straddle the hangars. By this time the AA had opened up and feeling one or two nearby bursts, I zoomed up 500ft and quickly shook them off. I was up to 10,000 in about two minutes and from there to 16,000 took under seven minutes. I decided to test her ceiling on the way home. I was climbing at 800 feet per minute at 18,000, but at 18,800 the altimeter jammed. Climbing hard for another ten minutes, I reckoned I must have added another 4–5,000 feet the fact that on throttling down it took over five minutes descending at between five and ten degrees before the altimeter started dropping. Five minutes at more or less maximum height, without oxygen and in an open cockpit at 6 am was as much as I could stick — I was puffing like a grampus! I passed directly over Knocke, Zeebrugge, Ostend and Westende at 17-18,000ft and was heavily shelled by them all. Knocke putting up some of her 9in bursts quite near enough, but I had only to do a 3-400ft zoom and steady climb and they seemed unable to keep pace with me. On the way down I tested her climb from 4,000 to 9,000 feet which she did in four minutes and fifteen seconds. Landed at 7.5 am having been in the air two hours and fifteen minutes.

I spent much of the afternoon writing a report on the Hispano Sopwith N50 and its suitability for operational work. Despite its speed and excellent climb, I had to criticize its poor manoeuvrability and extremely heavy lateral control. Also the cockpit being under the centre section meant that the pilot, whilst having good visibility forward and downward, was vulnerable to attack from above and as a single-seater bomber would need to be escorted.

John Fowler (Intelligence) interrogated me on my observations on Gontrode and seemed well satisfied with the information I was able to give him. A wonderfully clear day and a lovely evening. My head rather bad as a result of the prolonged high altitude. Chadwick shot down a three-seater into the sea early this morning and Huskisson's squadron got another three-seater at 7 pm. Very many EA were reported seen early this morning, apparently intending to waylay us on our return, but they were evidently too late.

26 May

Up at 3.20 am for another raid on St Denis Westrem. Clarke, Jope and Cooke with St John and gunlayers on DH4s and myself on the N50, but all turned back off Westende on account of extremely bad visibility. I had to nurse my engine very carefully on the way back as owing to a water leak she lost all her water and very nearly seized. Later two 1½ Strutters with Le Pecq bombs and two DH4s escorted Handley Pages on a hostile shipping patrol, enemy destroyers being reported off Nieuport. Two destroyers were sighted about twenty miles out to sea off La Panne and these opened fire on our machines, which, however, did not retaliate under the impression they were friendly craft. So far it has not been discovered whether they were allied or hostile. I took Jope up in N5221 after tea and, after circling over Bergues and the docks, we visited Bray Dunes and came down to 200ft over the front at La Panne where Jope tested the Lewis guns out to sea which alarmed many bathers who came tumbling out of the water apparently under the impression that we were an enemy aircraft. Back along the beach at 20-50ft, crossing the docks at 1,000 and landing at 7.30 pm — an enjoyable flip.

27 May

Whit Sunday. A short service at 9.45 am. Very warm and thick haze. Three of us left at 6.15 pm for St Denis. My water connection burst out to sea off Westende and for fifteen seconds I was enveloped in steam and nearly cooked! Turned back and again with no water in the radiator, had to nurse the N50 very carefully, just making the aerodrome with a violently hot engine. Clarke and Cooke returned at 8 pm, having bombed hostile shipping moored along the Zeebrugge Mole, the visibility being too bad and the wind too strong to continue to Ghent.

Cooke claimed a direct hit on a submarine which must have been sunk or heavily damaged. Enemy aircraft in force at 11 pm, many heavy explosions in the docks area. Stewart of 2 Squadron missing since yesterday. He was last seen over Nieuport.

28 May

I attended a French funeral in Dunkirk at 8 am. Paul Bewsher was there in charge of the Coudekerque party. Glaisby and observer and Robertson with Chase landed on DH4s at 11.15 to escort us to St Denis Westrem. We all left (Le Mesurier with St John, Jope with Darby on DH4s and myself solo on N50) at 12.30 pm. Following the coast well out to sea, we observed two destroyers and two submarines making for Ostend, and a further destroyer entering the Mole. We turned inland over the Dutch frontier and arrived over Ghent at 1.50 at 15,000 ft in good formation. Visibility good in spite of much cumulus at 10,000ft. I dropped in two runs over the target at 12,000 and 11,200 but could not observe results. St John obtained two direct hits on the large hangar and Jope another with a 112pdr. Eight very large white planes were scattered about the aerodrome and many bombs were seen to drop near and amongst them and must have caused considerable damage. We circled after dropping and, quickly picking up formation, headed for home via Thourout and Dixmude, getting a good view of the crumbled remains of the latter. I climbed to 19,000 over Dunkirk, from 15,000 to 19,000 taking just four minutes. Landed at 2.50 pm. Our two escorts did not keep up with us on the return flight when they were most needed. Glaisby lost himself flying south of Ypres and striking the coast at Boulogne! Ormerod and Dickson carried out their first flights on DH4s successfully. It transpires that Nungesser followed us over to Ghent and had a scrap with four EA between Ghent and Bruges, one of them driving him down from 14,000 to 4,000ft and making rings around his 160hp Nieuport which was badly shot about. He delights in lone expeditions.

The 'eight very large white planes' were the first of the Gothas. Only three days before the 'England' Squadron of 24 Gotha IVs had been formed for daylight bombing of London. The twin-engined aircraft, with a crew of three and bomb-load of 1,000lb, were, in spite of their speed, a mere 80mph, well armed and difficult to shoot down. By September counter-measures forced the Germans to switch to night attacks. 230 were built.

30 May

A dud day with clouds at 1,000ft. Rouse, Chadwick, Thom, Hamilton and Gow came to dinner. A full-out evening. Gow waxed eloquent on his usual topic — 'the hard lot of the down-trodden Observer'. A rough-house at 11.30 pm, originating in our cabin but finally carried into the 'enemy's' camp when Jope and I invaded Le Mesurier's and, the door being locked and barricaded, an entry was more or less effected through the roof.

31 May

A fine morning but strong west wind. Clarke, Ormerod, Cooke and I left for St Denis at 1 pm, but visibility being poor and thick clouds having obscured the mainland, we turned back off Flushing and bombed the Mole and three destroyers just off its northern end, which quickly got under way and zig-zagged out to sea, several bombs falling alongside them. Good formation up and back, all landing safely at 3.15 pm. Gardener returned from leave so I suppose my spell on N50 is ended? Ten Handley Pages and all the Shorts are raiding tonight, weather permitting — some twelve tons of explosive should shake the enemy a bit! We were shaken out of our beds at 12 pm by eight very heavy explosions but whether EA or a Short or a Handley Page dropping bombs out to sea owing to engine trouble I don't know. 'Mournful Mary' the Dunkirk warning siren, did not sound and there were no AA or searchlights.

> The Short Bomber first appeared in 1916 as a torpedo seaplane, one of which carried out the only aerial reconnaissance during the Battle of Jutland. Top speed of the bomber was a mere 77mph. Apart from the RNAS, a small number of Shorts were flown by the RFC in the Battle of the Somme.

1 June

Le Mesurier, Dickson and Cooke left on DH4s to raid St Denis. Gardener got away twenty minutes later on N50, the Hispano Sopwith, but returned having failed to pick up the formation as far as Zeebrugge.

2 June

A Hun paid us a visit at 4.30 am and was seen clearly at about 5,000ft. The AA actually put up some good shooting for a change. Jope went on leave by the 9 am destroyer. I am down for a moonlight stunt early tomorrow and a daylight one later.

3 June

The King's birthday. Moonlight stunt washed out, but at 4 am Le Mesurier, Gardener, Dickson and I left on DH4s for Bruges docks. Strong west wind took us to our target by 4.30. Here things became very lively, the AA being heavy and uncomfortably close. After our first run over the target my gunlayer, Sambrook, signalled a second run as he had not got all his bombs off, so rather unwillingly I turned for a second run. By the time we had completed this our other three aircraft were out of sight on the way home, but Sambrook scored a hit on a vessel in No. 1 dock. Every battery was now concentrated on us and we were continually bracketed fore and aft, on both flanks, above and below, and turn, twist, zoom and sideslip as I did, I could not shake them off and thought every next salvo would get us. We were surrounded by the acrid smoke of near misses and several times our old DH4 was tossed bodily by the blast. At last, after what seemed an eternity, but was I suppose only a matter of ten minutes, the shelling suddenly ceased and, for a moment, I comforted myself with the thought that they had tired of wasting ammunition on me. My complacency only lasted a few seconds before violent signals from Sambrook indicated danger below and, banking sharply, I saw a small vicious aircraft hurtling up at us at great speed. We were doing over 90 knots but he fairly streaked up to us and had us utterly outclassed for both speed and climb. He opened fire from about a hundred yards and went on firing to within some twenty-five yards, coming at us diagonally from the rear and above and trying at first to get under our tail and between us and the sun, but this I kept him from doing.

In his first attack a bullet whizzed about an inch in front of my face shattering to fragments my starting mag. switch on the dashboard and passing out through the side cowling; further bullets passed through struts and planes and one through a cartridge in the belt of my starboard gun — my port gun jammed from the first. Sambrook, however, was blazing away like mad with the back gun. In spite of this the hun dived on us three times, his speed being so great that after delivering each attack he was away out of range before diving on us again. His three attacks were delivered within five minutes.

Meanwhile I was swinging the machine about and making for the Lines nose down for all I was worth, but with a stiff wind against us it seemed he must get us with one of his lightning dives. However, after his third attack he sheared off evidently having had enough lead from Sambrook who had poured 3 trays off at him. I could see our tracers passing through his V-Strutter Albatros and could see his head clearly and almost his expression as he turned away. He may well have been wounded but we could not claim him. Altogether I don't want to experience such another strafing, but a miss is as good as a mile and I've got one or two souvenirs out of it. Le Mesurier dived on one he saw and thinks he got him as he went down in a series of stalls and spins, and we saw another dive vertically leaving a trail of smoke but he flattened out low down. My DH4 required quite a lot of attention before it flew again. Most of the squadron went over to Wing HQ later in the morning to hear Mr Handley Page lecture on 'The performance of aircraft in relation to power and loading'. He managed to work quite a lot of humour into his talk. Played in a cricket match in the afternoon, my contribution being 7 runs.

4 June
Six of us on 1½ Strutters (Clarke, Gardener, Le Mesurier, Wright, Cooke and myself) left at 1.45 am for St Denis. Followed coast up to Blankenberghe and then turned in, skirting Bruges which put up a blaze of AA and flaming onions. I couldn't see the Bruges–Ghent canal but the Scheldt was visible in the moonlight and with compass aid I was able to spot Ghent docks at 2.35 am and, coming down to 4,000ft, hit off the aerodrome after a five minute search, the woods on either side and the white road across it showing up clearly. Loosed off my bombs from 3,000 on a good line at 2.50 am and, the old Clerget picking up well, was soon passing over Thielt steering due west for the Lines. Visibility was good and I could dimly see the coast some thirty miles to my north soon after leaving Ghent. The Dutch islands showed up very clearly and I could see the lighthouses flashing somewhere up by the Zuider Zee. Passing over Roulers I headed for a colossal strafe which was going on just south of Ypres and which I had observed on the outward journey along the coast. Throttling down, I circled for some time over the Ypres Salient at 12,000. Guns were flashing in every direction, thousands of them, and numbers of huge red flares lit up the darkness below. I had not realized that at that height I might well be in the line of trajectory of big shells passing to and fro until a violent bump, which could have been nothing else than the disturbance caused by a large one passing close, warned me to clear off, which I did without delay. With such a strafe going on, thousands of shells a minute must have been pouring through the air at all heights. From Ypres I passed over Poperinghe and, still having time to waste before daylight, did a little tour round Cassel, St Omer and Watten before landing at 4.15 am. Altogether a priceless raid. Le Mesurier and Gardener failed to find the target. Turned in at 5.30 am and slept or dozed until 11.30.

Enemy aircraft paid us a visit last night and a large number of heavy bombs were dropped on the Depot and St Pol aerodromes and several in a field away from us. The place fairly shook so that we got next to no sleep at all, being up at 1 am for our raid. After lunch Wright and I went to the Depot and saw where five large bombs had cratered the aerodrome, wounding four ratings, one of whom has since died. Many also dropped at St Pol making craters 20ft in diameter. Teddy Gerrard did some very pretty spins, side-loops and cartwheels on a Triplane, after dining with us on his way to Coudekerque.

5 June

Enemy aircraft over again by 11 pm last night and plenty of bombs dropped. AA very active. The ship's bell sounded 'Dug-outs' but I was too tired to respond seeing that we were being called at 1 am. Six of us (Gardener, Wright, Omerod, Dickson, Cleghorn and myself) took off at 2 am for Bruges on Sopwiths, Clarke with Garret also, on a DH4. AA and searchlights intensely active. I approached the target, the submarine depot on the docks, at 5,000ft amidst a goodly display of fireworks, flaming onions in huge long chains being much to the fore. Several HE bursts close but no damage and, having dropped my load on a good traverse, I decided to shoot up some of the searchlights at Zeebrugge on my way back. Shutting off, I endeavoured to dive down the beam but had to push the old Sopwith to well over 100 knots before I could get my sights anywhere near. I began to regret my enterprise after firing a short burst as the beggar got full on to me, as did several others, and I was illuminated like a moth in a headlight and for all my dodging could not shake them off, the HE following swiftly and I felt many bursts far too close for comfort. Eventually I got out of range and, speeding back along the coast, landed at 4 am.

Omerod lost his engine and overshot, landing in a field. On touching ground a 65lb bomb which had hung up in its rack dropped off and was detonated by the tail skid striking the detonator needle. Fortunately it proved to be a very dud bomb, merely blowing off much of the tailplane, tearing a large hole in the top of the fuselage, a large piece flying past Omerod's head and shoring through the top starboard plane. Garrett's remark on Omerod walking to the Mess carrying large fragments of the bomb in his arms was, "What the blazes are you doing here? You ought to be in hell." A lucky let-off indeed. Bombs did occasionally hang up and, if one knew this had happened, the usual course was to fly well out to sea and, by violent stunting, try to shake them off. In the afternoon the King of the Belgians accompanied by various dignitaries carried out an investiture at Coudekerque. Wing Captain Lambe received the Order of Chevalier of the Légion d'Honneur and Spenser Grey and Newton Clare were made Companions of that Order. The King then inspected the station and, after tea, went up in a Handley Page piloted by Babington, Buss taking up the lesser lights in a second HP. Clarke, Gardener and Le Mesurier patrolled over them in two Triplanes and a Camel, doing many loops.

6 June

A much-needed pukka night's rest at last, the weather preventing a moonlight raid. At 12.30 pm Le Mesurier, Clarke, Dickson and I left on DH4s for Houttave aerodrome, Dickson dropping out early with engine trouble. Followed coast, turning in over Wenduyne, and got a good line over the target, Darley observing our stick of bombs hit the large hangar and also observing a further hit, apparently one of Le Mesurier's bombs. Severe strafing from Blankenberghe's batteries which shelled us accurately until five or six miles out to sea. Very hot and hazy. The RNAS has accounted for eight out of eighteen big Gotha machines which raided England yesterday.

7 June

Six of us flew over to Coudekerque on 1½ Strutters to fly before the King and Queen of the Belgians, the King having apparently so enjoyed his last flight in a Handley Page that he wants to take his Queen also! I took Le Mesurier over in N5150. The royal party arrived at 5.10 and were received by Lambe, and 5 Squadron's pilots presented, the King shaking hands and having a word or two to say. Afterwards the Queen did likewise and asked us to pose while she took a photograph, in due course sending each of us a copy. At 5.30 six of us in good formation kept up a patrol over the aerodrome while the royal party had tea, and later escorted them while they were aloft in the Handley Page piloted by Babington. Sharman of 10 Squadron landed at Coudekerque on a Triplane very badly shot up this morning. He was driven down by a swarm of Huns many miles over the Lines and hedge-hopped home at a height of 20-30ft dodging trees and other obstacles and pursued by numerous enemy as far as the Lines. Gardener, flying N50 back to England, suffered a seized engine and only just made Folkestone aerodrome.

8 June

Hazy all the morning with rain after tea. The papers brought good news tonight, the Ypres Salient having been flattened out and Wytscheate and Messines captured, together with over 5,000 prisoners. The advance was preceded by a huge mine explosion, 450 tons of Amatol being touched off. That accounts for the heavy strafes we have been hearing for some days and what I witnessed on the night of 3 June, returning from the St Denis Westrem raid. The guns are thundering like mad again tonight.

6

The Leugenboom Gun

With the arrival of our first DH4s in May and early June, 1917, and the gradual phasing out of our old Sopwith 1½ Strutters, 5 Squadron became a pure day bomber squadron and, from 5 June onwards, with one exception on 13 July, no more night raiding was carried out. By the beginning of July we mustered five DH4s and were able to carry out a number of effective day missions. The DH4 was well adapted for day bomber work, capable of carrying a 450lb bomb load and, with an observer or gunlayer in the back handling twin Lewis guns on a Scarff mounting, had good protection. The pilot had twin synchronized Vickers guns firing forward through the propeller arc. Originally fitted with the 250hp Rolls Royce Eagle VI engine, later models had the 275hp Eagle VII and, finally, the 375hp Eagle VIII; the last giving a top speed of around 130 knots and a ceiling of some 22,000 feet. Our early DH4s, however, hardly exceeded 110 knots and we had difficulty in getting them above 15,000 with bombs, but they handled well and the Rolls Eagle VI proved wonderfully reliable. An effective bomb sight enabled precision bombing to be carried out by the observer or gunlayer who steered the pilot over the target by means of string 'reins'. This was the only means of communication between the rear man and the pilot.

9 June
Le Mesurier, Dickson, Cleghorn and I left at 1.15 pm for St Denis Westrem on DH4s, McSorley being my gunlayer. Good formation maintained to the Schelde. Big cloud banks by then obscured the ground and we had a fifteen-minute search at 14,000 ft before sighting Ghent and, by a stroke of luck, I sighted our target and McSorley loosed off our bombs at 12,000, though on account of clouds and haze it was impossible to see results. Quickly I regained formation and maintained it closely on return by Eccloo, Bruges and Dixmude. Shelled by the last two but nothing very close. On landing found both blades of my propeller badly split, presumably by the long grass taking off as Dickson had suffered in the same way. That accounted for the slight vibration and whistling sound I had noticed. Four Shorts landed prior to a night raid on Houttave aerodrome.

14 June

Very hot but extremely thick weather has kept us grounded for several days, but we have relieved the monotony by bathing at St Malo, visits to the Hotel des Arcades, etc and on the 11th several of us spent the day at Boulogne. Wright is transferred to Manston, much to his disgust, and left on the 9 am destroyer. In the evening I took up A. M. Butcher in N5150 to test his capabilities as a prospective gunlayer. I flew him along the Lines by Dixmude and Ypres. A very clear evening. The whole country south of Ypres is torn up for a huge area as a result of the recent offensive and presents the appearance of a sand desert, with not a patch of green for miles and miles. Jope and I dined with Tommy and 'Pin' at Malo and afterwards strolled along the beach. A perfect evening. Jope and I walked back across the fields.

15 June

Five of us left at 9.10 am for St Denis, Le Mesurier leading, myself with Sambrook on left, then Cleghorn, Jope and Dickson. Good formation going and returning. Usual route and back by Bruges, Thourout and Dixmude. Dropped at 13,000, Sambrook observing both our 112lb bombs strike a hangar which belched forth smoke and flame. AA over Ghent very heavy and at our level but owing to the thick haze they probably did not see us clearly as none of us were hit. I saw three enemy scouts slightly above our level as our formation was reassembling but these made no attempt to attack. Landed at 11.55. Dickson lost his engine and came down in the sea half a mile out from Malo. As he was with us at 16,000 over Nieuport, strange he couldn't pull off a landing on the sands. Garrett, Jope and I went down to see the salvage and then had a glorious bathe, Jope and I continuing to Dunkirk for tea at Goberts.

16 June

Extremely hot — 105 degrees. Standing by all day for a raid which didn't come off, being finally washed out at 5 pm after I had tested conditions as far as Coxyde with Jope as passenger. Very thick haze and clouds over Belgium. Jope and I walked towards the Fort after dinner to find a bathing pool he'd spotted from the air; found it and he thereupon undressed and sampled it and was quite pleased with the result in spite of a muddy bottom.

17 June

Jope, Cleghorn, Omerod and I left at 8.40 am for Bruges docks. Followed coast to near Dutch frontier before turning inland. Burdett, my gunlayer, steered me a good course over the target where we dropped one 65lb and 12 x 16lb and observed many explosions amongst shipping in the western basin and on the quayside where a wood stack was set ablaze. AA very heavy but, as far as I was concerned, not very accurate, haze probably handicapping the gunners. Passed within 500 yards of two large enemy two-seaters proceeding in the opposite direction, but though we were alone at the time they took no notice of us and, our instructions as bombers being to return without looking for trouble, we left them alone. Many more hostile aircraft observed lower down. Heat all day was intense – 110 degrees. On my way back from Bruges, Nungesser came and stunted around me in his Nieuport off La Panne, his vivid stripings and skull, crossbones, coffin and candlesticks showing up very vividly.

18 June
A very grilling morning, hotter than ever. A terrific storm blew up in the afternoon, preceded by fifteen minutes of the worst dust storm I've ever seen, the wind suddenly rising to hurricane fury. It passed quickly and at 6 pm Le Mesurier, Jope, Gardener and I went down to a pool we had prospected from the air and had a ripping dip. The water was very warm and a bridge gave us a six-feet dive. Jope and Gardener went down again at 10 pm and bathed in the glare of vivid and incessant lightning. Another big storm at 11 pm.

19 June
Still very close and warm after thunderstorms all night. After tea test flights for prospective gunlayers to observe shipping in the docks. Le Mesurier and the CO got away at 5.30 and I should have followed but for a dud engine. Big thunderstorm coming up. Le Mesurier got down just in time but the CO landed in deluges of rain and violent thunder and lightning fifteen minutes after the storm started – ten minutes later it would have been impossible for a machine to have lived in it. Jope and several others went bathing again at 10 pm.

20 June
Very hot again and big storms hovering around. After lunch we all went to the Depot to examine a captured Albatros scout and witness its performance against a Camel and a Triplane. Casey flew the Albatros (160 hp Mercedes), Le Mesurier the Triplane and Allen the Camel. The Albatros was outclassed for speed and climb but manoeuvred well and doubtless in the hands of an Albatros expert would have shown up better. She is very much on the lines of a Nieuport but more heavily

loaded, fuselage in three-ply throughout and finely streamlined. Guest night with five officers from the Royal West Yorks and a Frenchman who played the 'cello magnificently.

> By January, 1917, all 37 'Jastas' at the Front were equipped with the V-strutter Albatros DIII and for the next six months they swung the balance of air superiority in Germany's favour. The sesqiplane design was inspired by the success of the Nieuport fighters.

21 June
Overcast morning. I took A. M. Butcher up in Sopwith N5221 at 11.45 for gunlayer training. Gave him ten minutes over the docks which were very full of shipping, and then climbed through a layer of clouds at 3-4,000ft for another layer which completely overcast the sky, but these proved to be at 18,000 and I didn't get there. Good views of Ypres etc. Held the nose up and stopped the propeller on the way down. Gliding with it stationary at 50 knots, the air was particularly still and it was quite easy to talk to Butcher in the back seat and to hear sounds coming from the ground. Large number of kite balloons seen. After lunch nine of us left by tender for Cassel, a run through nice country and up the winding ascent to the top of the hill on which it is perched. From there we pushed on through Abeele to Poperinghe and thence through the shell-torn village of Vlamertinghe to within a mile of Ypres, where the bursting of large numbers of shells on either side of the road 2-300 yards ahead brought us to a standstill by a much battered house just past the railway crossing. There lay the remains of a transport lorry which we subsequently learned had received a direct hit this morning. Jope, Omerod and I walked some little way further up the road towards Ypres, a holocaust of torn and shattered trees and shell craters on either side. Some soldiers popped up from a dugout alongside the road and persuaded us not to risk it any further, and as several heavies burst across the road 200 yards beyond the point we reached a minute or two later, maybe it was as well we took their advice, though it was disappointing when so near not to get into the town. Large numbers of our own 18lb shells complete in cases, wicker baskets and all, were strewn on either side of the road and Jope and I were anxious to collect several and bring them along to disarm at leisure, but the others were 'windy' so we regretfully left them, though with fuses set to safe they would have been quite harmless, however bumpy the road, and McSorley could have disarmed them. Army traffic had been very heavy around Poperinghe but the sudden cessation of all traffic for the last mile or so we covered

seemed a bit uncanny. A good tea in Cassel at the Sauvage which commands a magnificent view over the rolling country towards Béthune and Arras. Another terrific storm blew up and delayed our departure and we eventually landed back at 7.45 pm wet through after a thoroughly interesting and enjoyable afternoon 'seeing the war'.

23 June
A fine breezy morning with huge cumulus clouds. I took Jope up in N5221 around Dunkirk and Bergues and then climbed through the clouds in the direction of Cassel. Struck clouds at 4,000 and never saw such magnificent ones. For some time we succeeded in threading a path through gaps and valleys with enormous masses towering up on either side and almost brushing our wingtips — a really wonderful and extraordinarily beautiful sight. Finally a huge mass blocked our way and for five or six minutes we were buffeted by terrific bumps and with no horizon to guide one the air speed rushed up and then fell most alarmingly — at one time we were hanging by our belts. At length I managed to get her level and, climbing hard, emerged into dazzling sunshine again with gorgeous cloud panorama at 9,000ft, huge white masses still towering up for thousands of feet above us, and many gaps showing up the sun-girt villages and woods below; while far out to our north lay the deep blue of the Channel with the cliffs of Dover and Folkestone, and all Thanet stretching away on the horizon. Quite the most beautiful view I have ever had. I stopped the propeller on the way down and glided very gently and silently for a while taking in the glory of it all. Jope took a number of cloud photographs. Tea at Goberts in the afternoon, meeting many from other squadrons. Clouding up threateningly again. Two joy-riding Shorts arrived for our use.

24 June
Sunday and a short service at 10 am. Burrows and I walked to the chateau at 11 am and met several of the Royal West Yorks officers who showed us round the place, their tents, horses and so on.

27 June
Awakened at 5 am by heavy detonations occurring regularly every eight minutes which Jope and I took to be AA practice as distant explosions followed at regular seventeen-second intervals. On getting up, however, it proved to be a 15-inch gun strafing Dunkirk from long range. The distant lighter explosion we had taken for AA shells bursting high up, was the actual sound of the gun firing, the shell outpacing the sound of the gun by seventeen seconds. One of the first shells landed on Malo

Casino, another did extensive damage to the seaplane base, killing five ratings. They then concentrated on Coudekerque, the Handley Page squadron evidently being their target. Le Mesurier went up with Jope on N5150 and counted thirteen craters in the vicinity of Coudekerque, three being on the aerodrome, another shell falling while they were overhead at 5,000ft, at which height they felt the bump quite distinctly. I went up later with Nash in the back and counted fourteen, while the nearby farm was blazing, the buildings being completely wrecked. An enormous smokescreen blocked out Ostend and district. The shelling ceased at midday. After lunch I flew the big Short over to Coudekerque – a huge unwieldy aircraft compared with the 1½ Strutter, tail-heavy and very tiring to fly. After tea I had a look at the craters, huge affairs 30ft across and 15ft deep, but their effect seems to have been very local as the shells falling from extreme altitude penetrated deeply into the soft ground before exploding. A base plate of one had been recovered and it alone must weigh 200lbs. Fortunately no damage to our buildings or aircraft.

This was the Leugenboom gun situated in a wood some miles inland from Ostend, which soon became a target for the Handley Page squadron. It was firing at 27½ miles' range.

29 June

12 Squadron arrived at Petite Synthe from St Pol and are accommodated in Bessoneaux hangars on the south side of the aerodrome. Commanded by Squadron Commander E. W. Norton and including Everett and eleven Flight Sub-Lieutenants, the majority of whom flew over their Pups, Triplanes and Camels. A disastrous start-off; one Triplane touched down in the wheat and turned a somersault, the pilot fortunately escaping unhurt, but Tulley on a Camel, after doing several side-loops and rolls ridiculously low down, failed to recover from a spin and crashed very badly on the railway track. He was just alive when we reached him and got him on a stretcher but died as we carried him along the line. Alas, a case of over-confidence and inexperience – he had only been out a fortnight and done some 40 hours flying. He should have become a brilliant pilot but recklessness cost him his life. I flew Jope over to Coudekerque after lunch and stayed to tea. Afterwards, together with Victor Sieveking examined craters in the surrounding fields and blitzed farm. The gun has now been located at Leugenboom and photographed. It is in a wood 27 miles from Dunkirk and our Handley Pages will bomb it. The shells took 1 minute 34 seconds coming.

30 June

A thoroughly wet day. After lunch Clarke, Thom, St John, Jope and I left in the box tender for Ypres. The others got off at Poperinghe, Jope and I continuing to Ypres. Left the car beyond Vlamertinghe and walked along the battered road into Ypres past many interesting sights and the ruins of an asylum. As shells were continuously raining into the centre of the town, their overhead scream being loud and frequent, we could not reach the square and explore the Cloth Hall, contenting ourselves with walking through a few streets levelled to the ground and exploring a huge crater just outside the town where the Germans had scored a direct hit on a 6in howitzer and its ammunition store, much of which had evidently gone up, the gun itself flung from its carriage and mounting, the twisted remains of which were in the bottom of a 30ft deep crater with 6in shells hurled in every direction. On our way back we managed to heave three complete cases of 18lb shells on to the car together with other souvenirs, picked up the other three in Poperinghe and drove on to Cassel with Jope and I sitting on the fuses. We had an excellent dinner at the Sauvage and reached Petite Synthe at 9.30 complete with loot.

1 July

Frightfully fed up. The promotion list out and I'm not on it nor any of the Flight Sub-Lieutenants either here or at Coudekerque, though numbers at home who have seen little or no active service have got their second 'ring' many of them junior to ourselves. A beastly shame. As usual the slackers at home with cushy safe jobs have got everything. It's too sickening. I wouldn't change with them anyway. Jope, Garrett and I spent the afternoon and evening up to dinner disarming 18lb shells in the armoury — an interesting job.

2 July

A fine morning with strong north-east wind. Clarke, Jope, Dickson, Cleghorn and I left at 11.40 am for Bruges docks but were attacked off Blankenberghe by numerous enemy fighters which had been shadowing us all the way from Westende. We were forced to drop our bombs out at sea and fight a rearguard action. Fortunately our formation was good and close so that none ventured to dive down into our midst, hanging above and behind us instead, ready to pounce on any straggler. Sambrook, my gunlayer, put up good shooting and one that attacked us went down in a vertical nose dive but we were unable to follow him down as a second took his place and needed all Sambrook's attention. Their shooting was poor and they never attempted to close on us as did the one that attacked us on 3 June. Two EA were over Petite Synthe at 3.30 pm and showed up very clearly against high cirrus clouds. They treated the AA, which as usual was very wide, with supreme contempt. None of our aircraft were up at the time though several took off at once from St Pol.

3 July

Le Mesurier, Dickson, Jope, Cleghorn and Burrows left for Lichtervelde ammunition dump at 12.15 pm — my first stand-off since 1 June. Cleghorn lost formation over the floods and did not reach the objective. AA reported not very abundant, but what there was was very accurate. Jope's machine holed in three places and he himself hit by a spent piece of HE on the shoulder. I took N5150 over to Bray Dunes after tea, seeing Shook, Rouse, Chadwick, Enstone and others. On leaving my engine seized at 1,500ft and I had to land on the sands a mile east of Malo. I got her pegged down by 10pm and an army guard set over her, returning to Petite Synthe at 10.30 pm. Le Mesurier landed in almost the same spot with the same trouble last night. Enemy aircraft dropped three bombs on Bray Dunes last night and several more off the aerodrome. The Leugenboom gun put over four more 15in shells this afternoon which dropped in the sea opposite the Red hospital.

4 & 5 July

Unsettled and much rain. Jope, Burrows and I spent some time disarming 18lb shells. The Fleet Paymaster came in at 10.30 am on the 5th. I drew 15 francs, expecting about 300, and they made poor old Garrett's pay to be a minus quantity! Jope drew 450 — the ways of 'The Pay' are weird! After tea I went down with Le Mesurier and we landed on the sands near my N5150 which has had its seized engine replaced by a 130hp Clerget. The tide was fairly well out so I was able to take off into wind. A fine new engine — 1200 revs climbing and throttles beautifully. A nice evening above the clouds at 3,000.

6 July

Clarke, Sproatt, Cleghorn, McBain and I left at 4.30 for a raid on Ghistelles aerodrome. Good formation till off La Panne when McBain lost us and, later, Cleggy left us to open up on what he thought were attacking Huns, and we didn't see him again. The three of us carried on, being followed at a respectful distance by two who had shadowed us for a long time and were preparing to attack when AA opened up on us vigorously. They sheered off, leaving it to the guns. We got a good line over the target and Sambrook saw our 65lb strike one of the hangars and several of our smaller bombs fall amongst other sheds. St John, flying with Le Mesurier, got a direct hit on another hangar which belched smoke. AA heavy and accurate and many nasty black oily bursts of HE quite near enough.

7 July

A fine sunny day and very warm. I took St John up in N5152 at 3.45 pm to test weather conditions. Reported them good. Le Mesurier, Jope, Omerod, Wright and Burrows left at 5pm for Ghistelles. I went into town with McBain at 4.30 to see the damage done to the Malo Casino by the Leugenboom gun – a nasty mess. On return at 7 pm found our five DH4s had received a very hot welcome over the target by large numbers of Hun scouts. Wright had both rudder controls shot away on the starboard side, also a landing wire severed and many holes through fuselage, wings and tail. Omerod's petrol tank was pierced and oil sump holed, and Le Mesurier and Jope also collected a few holes. Edwards, Wright's gunlayer, was badly wounded in the thigh, taken out of the machine unconscious and succumbed half an hour later. Jope is promoted to Acting Flight Commander. No doctor on the Station as usual.

8 July

Heavy thunderstorms and wet or overcast all day. After lunch Cleghorn and I interrogated a Belgian suspect who spoke good English and had been found in a field by the military police, their suspicions being aroused by some questions he asked concerning troops passing through and by the fact that they understood him to say he was on leave, yet he was carrying amongst other kit a heavy automatic rifle. It was fairly evident, however, that he was a straggler from his regiment which was marching back for a rest from the trenches and, by reason of the weight he was carrying, had lagged behind and got out of touch and was merely enquiring as to their whereabouts. We handed him over to our military friends at the château who sent him, under escort, to the Base Commandant to be restored to his unit. After tea several of us left with Glaisby and his brother-in-law, a Major Hudson, to return him to his unit at Poperinghe. Dropping the major at Poperinghe, the rest of us carried on along the usual blitzed route into Ypres. Things seemed quiet so we drove the car right up to the asylum and walked on through streets of rubble to the square. Here the sight was amazing: hardly a house wall standing above the first storey and the shell-torn remains of the great Cloth Hall still looking stately and giving an impression of its former glory. Ypres, once a beautiful town, is now a mere shambles.

We continued to Cassel where we had again an excellent dinner at the Sauvage at 9.30pm, getting back to Petite Synthe at 11.15 pm.

9 & 10 July
Squadron Commander Bell, Collishaw and Sharman (3 Squadron) came over to tea, also Travers and Teddy Gerrard after much stunting low down on two Pups. Weather still dud, with very low clouds and a strong wind. A terrific strafe over Nieuport way at 11 pm. Enormous flashes and the glare of large fires. Awakened between 2 and 3 am by EA over Dunkirk and Bergues. Terrific bombardment lasted 20 minutes and sounded like destroyers.

This, although he did not know it, was a successful German surprise attack on the British XV Corps, 1st Division, two battalions being practically annihilated.

11 July
A lovely sunny day with light cumulus at 3,000ft. All our DH4s being out of action as a result of the strafing received over Ghistelles, the CO planned a day off to 'see the war'. Le Mesurier with Garrett and myself solo left in 1½ Strutters at 9.40 am and after flying at 1,500ft below cumulus clouds, we landed on Bailleul aerodrome at 10.20. A nice large aerodrome after our restricted one at Petite Synthe. Leaving our aircraft with No 1 Naval, we went up to their Mess, meeting their crowd. The CO with Newton-Clare in behind arrived shortly, while Cleghorn in the touring car went of to Poperinghe to collect the American Commander, Courtney. Garrett and I stayed to lunch while the others went off to join the rest of the party at Poperinghe. We saw three of our kite balloons brought down in flames by an EA which dodged out of the clouds and got them one after another, the occupants escaping in their parachutes.

Garrett and I left at 2.30 in a car to see the war, calling in at 1 RFC to collect Wright who, however, preferred to stay there and play tennis. The RFC have very snug quarters in a sort of garden city, numerous huts and glorified summer houses surrounding a lawn nicely laid out with flower beds. We drove by Locre and Kemmel to Messines Ridge and, leaving the car by the roadside, scrambled over shockingly torn and scarred country to our old reserve and front line trenches and on across former 'No Man's Land' to the old enemy trench system which was battered beyond recognition and could only be traced in places. We poked our heads into numerous more or less collapsed dugouts but were nearly overcome by the smell of rotting corpses — many gruesome sights which had not yet been cleared up. We visited the enormous mine craters made by the mine explosions reported to have been felt in London. They were some 100 yards in diameter and 70–80ft deep and, standing on top of the surrounding cone of earth, one got a good view of the rolling country about Messines which presents a picture of utter desolation. It being very clear, we could see Ypres, Armentières and other distant towns and for miles into enemy territory. High explosive and shrapnel were bursting persistently over a valley half a mile away where our 4.7s and 8in howitzers were steadily plugging away. We ran into the rest of our crowd who had come up from Poperinghe and all went back for tea at Bailleul, leaving at 7 pm for home. Le Mesurier flew the USA Commander back and, at his request, took him over Westende to give him experience of AA. A huge crowd for dinner and seven new arrivals for 12 Squadron.

12 July

Daly of 12 Squadron crashed badly on a Triplane this morning. Coming in at about 80 knots he hit the cornfield on the far side of the aerodrome, did a complete somersault over the road and finished upon his wheels, the fuselage from just behind his seat being doubled right under the undercarriage and the empennage being ahead of the engine. Incredibly he suffered nothing worse than a cut chin and bruised and cut knees. Immediately after that another 12 Squadron pilot on a Pup put the wind up everybody, having four attempts to land at about 70–80 knots and eventually narrowly escaping a crash. 12 Squadron must be averaging about a crash every flying day since they have been here. I think our aerodrome's limited size and perimeter hazards puts the wind up inexperienced pilots. Sproatt, Jope, Burrows and I had a lovely dip from the Malo beach after lunch. We had tea at Jope's 'find' in the Rue du Bassins and a second one at Goberts.

13 July

Moonlight stunt on Ghistelles early this morning in which Jope, Wright, Sproatt, Clarke and Burrows took part. Le Mesurier also went as a sort of excursion trip for the USA Commander who wanted to experience the thrills of a night raid. Le M gave him a few, taking four Le Pecqs with him over Ostend and getting held by the searchlights and heavily shelled, much to the Commander's delight. Wright had a very bad pile-up taking off. He swung badly and ran full-bore at about 50 knots into a stack of Bessoneaux framework, the front of the Sopwith 1½ Strutter was completely telescoped, the engine driven back on to the rudder bar which in turn was doubled up and pushed back almost on to the pilot's seat, the framework round the seat being reduced to matchwood. Wright, marvellously, escaped with only a bruise or two and climbed out of the wreckage and walked away. He was not strapped in and was flung upwards and forwards over the gun screen, thus saving his long legs which must otherwise have been badly smashed. All other aircraft returned safely, having received considerable help in finding the target by the enemy obligingly switching on landing lights as they approached, presumably thinking we were some of their own aircraft, which must have been out on a stunt or night practice. I collected a new DH4, N5996, from the Depot after tea – a lovely craft with a wonderful climb, the first 1,000ft almost in a zoom and the engine revving 1,700 climbing. Fowler (Intelligence) came over after dinner to describe to us a new and difficult objective for early tomorrow morning – Zedelghem ammunition dump, half-way between Bruges and Thouroult. It will certainly be difficult to find at night as there are no water or other landmarks near and one's only guide will be a main road and a railway, but it clouded up in the night and our stunt did not come off. St John has at last got his DSC.

14 July
Rain in the morning, clearing after lunch, when Commander Courtney and Garrett accompanied Clarke and myself to the Depot to collect two more DH4s. A storm delayed our departure but Clarke, with the Commander, got away at 4.45 pm and Garrett and I, after a cup of tea with Travers and Neville, at 5.30 pm. I let Garrett take control for ten minutes before landing at 6.10 pm. DH4, N5993 has a good performance but is a bad oil slinger. Commander Courtney left us after his entertaining visit, having sampled most experiences in pukka American style.

15 July
The Chaplain General, who arrived last night, gave us a stirring sermon. All leave washed out indefinitely – I had been hoping to go tomorrow! The CO, however, is going back to England for a month's sick leave being thoroughly run down. Squadron Commander S. J. Goble, DSC, is taking his place in the meantime. Heard that my promotion is now a cert, both SG and Lambe having put through a strong special recommendation, but I expect it will be weeks before it comes through.

17 July
Daly of 12 Squadron killed on a Camel, a repetition of Tully's crash –

stalling and spinning into the ground on a lefthand turn. Wild and Quinnett came round in the morning with the idea of getting joy rides, but seeing Daly's crash rather put them off. After lunch Omerod, Jope, Glaisby, Sproatt and I had a priceless bathe in the moat at Fort Ouest, a fine stretch of filtered sea water, warm and clear and 18–20ft deep, with a good diving board and a canoe to fool about in. The CO left for England and Goble arrived in his place. Some good tennis after tea.

20 July

After two days of impossible weather it cleared nicely, becoming fine and sunny with a stiff west breeze. At 11.15 Clarke, Sproatt, Glaisby, Cleghorn, Burrows and I left for a raid on Aertrycke aerodrome, just north of Bruges. Good formation and we picked up our escort of five RFC Bristol Fighters at 11,000 over Furnes. Crossed the Lines at 12,000 over Dixmude, our escort keeping well in the rear and far too high and, on being heavily shelled from Dixmude, took little further interest in us. Cleghorn was attacked from the rear whilst in good formation and his gunlayer, Burdett, severely wounded and his machine badly shot up, so that he had to turn for home then and there – the escort making no effort to drive off his attacker or to detail an escort for him on the way back. If his attacker had persisted he must have been shot down. On spotting the target I took a good line south to north over the aerodrome, our small bombs dropping amongst a group of scouts which must have suffered damage. By this time the rest of our formation were away to the east and immediately above me were three of the Bristols who should have been with the rest of the formation. They, however, turned for home and crossed the Lines well ahead of everybody! It seems they are unused to the heavy and accurate AA we experience in this part of the Lines. As it was, three more of our aircraft were attacked and badly shot up, Glaisby and two gunlayers being wounded and St John just grazed. Glaisby had a particularly narrow let-off, a bullet ripping through his helmet and causing a long gash on top of his head, fortunately not deep enough to damage the bone, another grazed his eye and shot the left-hand glass out of his goggles. Saw, his observer, although wounded in the forearm, fought his opponent for another ten minutes, eventually bringing him down – a remarkably plucky performance for his first time over the Lines. Clarke was attacked three times and riddled with bullets, his tank holed, a bullet grazed his shoulder, another just missed his knees knocking out the oil gauge and a third passing through his radiator. St John accounted for one EA. After tea several of us went down to St Pol and saw Clarke's machine, his tank was riddled and planes and fuselage full of holes, many made by explosive bullets.

21 July

Clouds at 800 in the morning but the sky cleared after lunch when another raid was planned. I was not down for it, but Burrows not feeling well, I took his place. Le Mesurier led off at 2.10 pm with Jope and Wright on his left and right, myself bringing up the rear. Picked up our escort of Biffs (Bristol F2b Fighters) over Furnes and this time they proved very efficient. Followed coast to Wenduyne and turned inland to find our target, Varssenaere aerodrome, five miles west-south-west of Bruges, without difficulty. Released bombs at 3.28 pm. Several of ours, including a 112lb, fell close to the line of hangars, some eight to twelve yards away and near enough to cause considerable damage. We all picked up formation very quickly after dropping and made for the coast, the escort keeping just above and behind us all the time. Heavy and fairly accurate AA from Bruges, Blankenberghe and Ostend until we were well out to sea. A few EA seen but low down and harmless. Formation wonderfully close and good on the return journey and escort perfect. An enjoyable raid and the presence of a good escort removed all anxiety. Did several stalls and cartwheels on the way back.

22 July

Fine, sunny day and very warm. Usual tennis after breakfast. Clarke, Sproatt, McBain, Burrows, Omerod and Garland took off at 12.20 pm for Varssenaere. All returned at 2.15 pm with the exception of Omerod, having been violently and accurately shelled. The RFC escort was again of little use and not seen at all on the return. Apparently two Flights escort us on alternate trips, one being good and the other much the reverse. Omerod eventually landed in two or three feet of water off La Panne, having been attacked over the target and his radiator pierced with the result that his engine seized and he lost formation. He was again attacked out to sea by three Albatros scouts and his machine badly shot up, but he just managed to make the coast off La Panne. His gunlayer, a new man, apparently had the wind up to such an extent that he was crouching down in his cockpit and never fired a single shot. Le Mesurier, Sproatt, Jope, England and I had a lovely dip in Fort Ouest moat, and Sieveking, Brackley, Weir and Johnson came over to tennis after tea. I took Lt Smith from the château up at 6.15 in N5081 for a joy ride along the coast. Visibility perfect and from Gravelines we could see the whole of the Kent coast and Thames estuary, the woods and hills showing up very clearly. Took N5081 up again at 7 pm for a short flight with Le Mesurier behind.

One cannot help remarking the sheer exuberance of so many of the pilots of the time. Leonard Rochford, a pilot in 3 Naval Squadron and close friend of my father, gives an account in his memoirs* of an Irishman, Francis Casey, who, while flying as an observer in a Nieuport two-seater had had his patience tested by his pilot's seeming reluctance to cross the Lines on a photographic mission over enemy territory, each time circling and turning back. "Now in the Nieuport two-seater the pilot's and observer's cockpits were not separated by a solid partition and the observer could stretch his legs under the pilot's seat. Casey waited until the pilot next turned towards the Lines and as soon as he reached them he pushed his leg under the pilot's seat and pressed his foot against the base of the control stick. The Nieuport started to dive and the more the pilot attempted to pull back the stick so Casey pushed his foot more firmly against it until the Nieuport steepened its dive to near vertical. Thinking something was wrong with the controls, the pilot became frantic and used all his strength to pull back the stick, but without success. At last when Casey judged the earth was rushing up towards them rather too quickly, he gradually decreased his pressure and the pilot was able to level out at about 100ft on the enemy side of the Lines. With perspiration streaming from his brow he turned westwards and headed for Dunkirk at full speed."

23 July

A hot and hazy day. Tennis after breakfast. Six of us left at 2.20 pm for a raid on Sparapellhoek aerodrome, but Garland and Wright returned with engine troubles. The rest of us got back at 4.15 pm having had a cinch of a raid, the haze being too thick for the gunners to see us clearly and no EA troubled us. Jope on the way back shot most of his propeller off testing his guns, the synchronizing gear having slipped. He consequently had to land on the beach at La Panne, damaging his chassis. Many officers of 55 Squadron, RFC paid us a visit from Boisdinghem and had tea, seeing over the station. They are a DH4 bomber squadron and apparently their aircraft have a better performance than ours as they never reckon to cross the Lines at under 15,000 and drop their bombs at 16–17,000ft, against our 11–12,000ft.

24 July

Very hot day and thick haze. Standing by all day for a raid but conditions impossible. Clarke flew me over to the Depot to bring back another DH4.

---

* *I Chose the Sky*, Leonard Rochford, DSC & Bar, DFC. William Kimber & Co, 1977.

25 July

I stayed in bed most of the morning feeling rather done, but as it rained hard I missed nothing. Weather cleared a bit after lunch, and by teatime patches of sky appearing so that at 5.30 pm five of us, led by Clarke, were able to take off for Houttave. Very good formation and picked up RFC escort over Furnes at 11,500ft. Crossed coast at Wenduyne being heavily but not accurately shelled. Target was very distinct and our bombs dropped alongside a large hangar, Darby (Sproatt's gunlayer) putting eight through its roof and setting it alight. Returned out to sea. Three scouts attacked our escort, which by the way was very good, on the way back and one of them was sent down in flames.

26 July

Clouds low and thick in the morning but cleared a bit after lunch. Five DH4s left at 2 pm in very doubtful weather for Vlisseghem aerodrome. All returned at 4.30 pm having had a comfortable trip, AA being unable to get a good line on them above the clouds and no EA seen. Garland got into a spin shortly after take-off but managed to pull out at 500ft above the ground. The Doc is recommending me for special leave on account of being run down. I am due for leave anyway. I was taking 9672 up for a test, but, on waving away chocks, I taxied slowly into another Sopwith which I had not noticed. Result, a broken prop and the Sopwith requires two new planes.

27 July

Another very hot day and large cloud masses at 2,000ft. Five of us, nevertheless, led by Clarke, left at 12.13 pm for Varssenaere aerodrome. Picked up escort at 12,000 over Furnes and, crossing the Lines at Dixmude, were lucky to spot the target through gaps in the clouds. Sambrook, my gunlayer, got a 65lb through the roof of one of the hangars on the east side of the aerodrome, close to the château. AA heavy but mostly wide on account of the clouds. A few Huns seen low down. Did some violent cartwheels over Furnes, leaving the seat once or twice, and then handed over control to Sambrook from Furnes and he flew remarkably well and could get us down all right, apart from the actual landing, if I was hit. My leave is sanctioned so I went over 'Hunland' in good spirits. Several of us bathed in Fort Ouest moat after tea. Terrific bombardment going on along the Lines in the evening.

> This was the preliminary counter-battery bombardment prior to the Allied offensive round Ypres, which was to drag on for four months until it became bogged down at Passchendaele.

28 July to 12 August
A Flight carried out their raid on Ghistelles and met with heavy shelling.
Wright's main spar was shot through in two places. Their air escort of
Bristol Fighters had a scrap with nine Huns, one of which was shot
down. I left at 4.30 pm for the destroyer, Le Mesurier, Jope and Sproatt
seeing me off. Beautiful crossing and sea like a millpond. We reached
Dover just too late to catch the London train, so spent the night at the
Grand and next day on to Swanage where my family were holidaying
together with sundry other relations. A bit of reaction set in and for a
while I felt very limp and run down, so that the local doctor who
overhauled me recommended a fourteen-day extension of my leave,
which in due course was approved. After indulging in much bathing and
cliff walking I reported back to Dover and found the destroyer had left
early, so went up to the aerodrome for lunch, and spent the afternoon
in Folkestone meeting some old friends. Crossed next morning in the
destroyer *Kangaroo* and reported to Wing headquarters at Malo for
interview by Captain Lambe. He was in very good humour and granted
an extension of leave until 4 September, the alternative being a medical
survey which would have meant my leaving his command and returning
to England – for which I had no wish. I lunched at HQ and then went
to Petite Synthe for the night, finding everyone much as usual and
working hard. Burrows has returned to England with heart trouble, and
Glaisby as a ferry pilot. Raids are being pushed off every possible day.
Soar, Enstone and Chadwick – the latter, alas, drowned when his Pup
hit a wave flying low over the sea, have been awarded DSCs, as well
as Sieveking, Roy Allan and Barker of 7 Squadron. Certain amount of
feeling here as the last two have only carried out some seven or eight
raids against 20 or 30 by many of us, Jope and myself having exceeded
30. Cleghorn, Potts and I are crossing by cruiser tomorrow. Le Mesurier
has been awarded a Bar to his DSC – damn well deserved. Another
gunlayer has been killed in a scrap during my absence. They seem to
get it worse than the pilots, being, I suppose, more exposed.

15 August to 3 September
The three of us left at 8.15 am and caught a drifter from the docks to
our cruiser, HMS *Active*, a four-funneller mounting ten 4in guns. We
were made very much at home by all and enjoyed our crossing, spent
on deck and in the Wardroom where we lunched in Dover harbour, a
great improvement on a destroyer. Wood and Soar took the destroyer
and travelled up to town with us. I caught the evening train from
Waterloo for Swanage but, missing the last connection at Wareham,
spent the night together with an army officer named Sims in the only

accommodation we could find — a double room at the Bear. Was in Swanage by 10 am next morning and found everyone much as I left them. Plenty of picnicking, bathing and tennis and on 23 August a telegram arrived from Le Mesurier telling me I had been awarded a DSC, and that Clarke had got a Bar to his. The last night of my leave spent at Broadstairs. A lovely moonlit night and Sissy and I walked down the front after dinner. Could see AA bursting clearly over Dunkirk and Bray Dunes which were being heavily bombed by the Huns. A Gotha wandered over and dropped a few pills out Reading Street way.

7

Against The Gothas

At the end of the summer of 1917 the naval squadrons at Dunkirk became engaged in tasks outside the purely naval requirements of the Dover Command – the bombing of submarine harbours, fleet reconnaissance and spotting for the monitors, and at Haig's request lent their support to the offensive in July known as the Third Battle of Ypres. It was Haig's plan to strike from the direction of Ypres towards Ostend and clear the sea flank, at the same time capturing the U-boat bases. This entailed attacking immensely strong positions along the Passchendaele ridge. Forty divisions were assembled.

Actually the Channel Ports were not indispensable to the conduct of the U-boat offensive, and the Admiralty misled Haig and Robertson on the importance of neutralizing them. The terrific artillery barrage opening the attack destroyed the drainage so that as winter approached the rains turned all into a sea of mud, which by the end of November had swallowed up 400,000 men. In Churchill's words, 'The full severity of a Flanders winter gripped the ghastly battlefield. Ceaselessly the Menin Gate of Ypres disgorged its streams of manhood.' It was 5 Naval's task to attack enemy airfields to keep down his reconnaissance aircraft, and to attack dumps and railheads.

4 September
At the end of a very good leave I reached Dover to find the destroyer had left at 11.30 am so, after spending the day at Folkestone and the night at the Langhorne Hotel, left in the destroyer *Kangaroo* at 1 pm, together with Huskisson and Enstone. A lovely day and nice crossing, much of the time spent on the bridge with the skipper, Lieutenant Commander Mansfield, RN. Reached 5 Squadron at 3.45 pm. All as usual, Jope on leave and Ruthven sick in England. Our RFC escort came to dinner. Gothas over from 9 pm till midnight, their fourth consecutive night visit. During my absence the enemy appear to have increased very materially their fighter strength, both numerically and in the quality of their pilots and, if yesterday's experience is a true sample and not just a flash in the pan, we seem likely to encounter really stiff opposition on future daylight raids. Yesterday, 3 September, an attempted raid on

Varssenaeres aerodrome was largely frustrated when our formation of eight DH4s was scattered by repeated attacks by large numbers of enemy fighters, despite the presence of our usual escort of 48 Squadron's Bristol Fighters. The latter accounted for two EA and all our eight DH4s returned safely though several were severely shot up, fortunately without casualties. One thing seems pretty certain – our repeated daylight attacks on enemy aerodromes has achieved one of its purposes, that of drawing off enemy fighters from, and relieving the pressure upon, the army front in Flanders.

9 September

I seem to have spent the last three days in bed, under Doc's orders, with a gastric attack. Fortunately dud weather and I have missed nothing. Eight DH4s left for Bruges at 11am, twelve Camels going with them in the hope of using them as 'bait'. DHs returned at 1 pm having been unable to find the target owing to very thick haze and clouds. I got up after lunch feeling a bit shaky but rapidly improved. Pownall crashed Le Mesurier's DH on landing after his first flight in one. An RFC Lieutenant came over in a Bristol Fighter after tea and tested it against Le Mesurier's DH, N6001. The DH slightly faster but outmanoeuvred and the Biff can dive at 200mph. He afterwards took Clarke and St John back to dine at the Frontier aerodrome, both in the back seat – some load!

10 September

Very vigorous enemy offensive started at 8.45 pm. Large number of bombs dropped between then and 11 pm, including many heavies. About half a dozen terrific explosions nearby. AA very active and many bits of shrapnel whistling around.

11 September

I was Raid Officer and up at 6.30 am. Twelve DH4s left at 9.40 for Sparapellhoek aerodrome, escorted by the usual RFC Biffs and fourteen Camels. I took Pownall up on N5974 at 10.45 am and gave him some dual instruction. Felt quite at home in the air after six weeks rest. Wandered around Calais, St Omer, Hazebrouck and Cassel and got the dud DH up to 15,000. Our DHs returned at 11.30. Le Mesurier was attacked by a scout who put an explosive bullet into the Lewis trays behind the observer's seat and set off some of the ammunition. The trays probably saved the gunlayer, who accounted for the Hun. Two more EA were brought down and one of the Biffs went down and failed to return. Five Red Cross nurses came over from Queen Alexandra

Hospital for tennis and tea. They were quite good fun. Three more came from La Panne as Norton's guests. Enemy aircraft over as usual at 8.40 pm but they didn't worry us.

12 September

Eight DH4s of A and C Flights left at 10 am for Bruges, with hostile shipping as an alternative objective. They bombed ships inside the Mole at Zeebrugge, being untroubled by EA and the AA was ineffective on account of cloud cover. Enemy aircraft arrived overhead again at 8.43 pm. Le Mesurier and Sproatt were active with our two mounted Lewis guns. At 9.30 one approached low down and released a very brilliant flare which lit up the whole area like day. Probably the tracers from our Lewis guns attracted him as he dropped a stick of six bombs across the aerodrome which flung up huge volcanoes of flame and sparks, but did no damage beyond leaving large craters to be filled in. The nearest fell within 25yds of 12 Squadron's tents and slightly wounded two Flight Sub-Lieutenants. Some scrum for the dugouts but didn't get in.

13 September

B and C Flights were to have left for a raid at 8 am, myself leading, but the weather turned dud with thick clouds all day and strong wind in the evening. Sproatt, Wright, McBain and I went into town at 3 pm for the weekly bath, afterwards having an excellent dinner at the Rue du Bassins.

14 September

Very cloudy early and strong wind, but, improving by 3 pm, B and C Flights took off for Bruges, myself leading the first formation and Le Mesurier the second. Good formation, but at 7,000ft over Gravelines Le Mesurier shot across my bows firing the washout signal, much to my disappointment as conditions really weren't too bad and I was anxious to carry through on my first occasion to lead a formation. So we all returned by 4 pm. Jope returned from leave and after tea he, Omerod, Shaw and myself went to the cinema in Malo and saw some quite good 'flicks'. Played snooker after dinner.

15 September

Heavy rain in the early morning, but cleared later and thirteen of us got away, in two formations, at 1 pm for a raid on Bruges with the usual alternative. I was on Jope's left in DH, N6000, in the front formation. We were at 13,000 over the usual meeting place, but Jope would not slacken speed sufficiently to let the formation close up, hence very straggly and the second formation never caught up. The usual escort of Biffs and Camels also were not with us. Observed several of our monitors, escorted by destroyers, some fifteen miles to sea off Ostend, putting up large smoke screens, presumably preparatory to bombarding Ostend. On account of very strong north-west wind, Bruges was abandoned and we attacked hostile shipping five miles off Ostend, many bombs falling near but no direct hits observed. On the way home I did a couple of spins, getting in about six turns and dropping 3,000ft. The DH4 spins rapidly, dropping its nose and gathering speed very quickly. We were round half a dozen turns in a matter of 15-20 seconds which nearly made Sambrook in the back seat sick. I afterwards dived her at 160 knots and was deaf for the rest of the day! Jope's and my own DSCs announced in the press — my own for bombing Houttave on 25 July, but I can't remember anything particularly meritorious about that raid. They now apparently have to specify some particular feat and not merely continuous good work.

16 September
A fine morning with a stiff west wind and light detached clouds at 2,000. Thirteen of us left in two formations at 10.30 for Bruges. I was in the second formation, Jope leading. Le Mesurier led the first. Picked up our escort of Biffs and Camels at 13,000 over La Panne and headed out to sea, our formation being somewhat in the rear of Le M's but steadily picking up. Then off Westende the whole of the front formation turned for home and, the raid being apparently washed out, our formation followed suit. Conditions were not unfavourable and, on landing, we discovered that both Le Mesurier and Sproatt had to fall out due to engine troubles and the remainder of their formation mistook the green Very light signals for white — a very deplorable mistake. The CO was very sick about the morning's fiasco and so detailed the leading Flight, who were to blame, for a repeat stunt. Sproatt and I also volunteered to go and so eight of us, led by Le Mesurier, took off at 3pm and, after picking up five Camels over Furnes, crossed the Lines just north of Dixmude and bombed Ghistelles. Two of our 65lb and eight 16lb just missed the hangars but a direct hit observed with a 65lb on a large red building just off the south-east corner of the aerodrome, thought to be the officers' quarters and Mess. AA very plentiful but no EA seen. I shut off over the floods and, diving down, fired a large number of rounds into the enemy trenches with my front guns. Sambrook followed suit with his Lewises.

17 September

Strong west wind all day so no flying. Brackley and Morrison came over for a court of enquiry on two ratings injured yesterday while swinging Omerod's propeller.

18 September

Rained hard all day. A 12 Squadron Flight Sub-Lieutenant severely injured in the morning by spinning a Pup into the ground from 150ft. Jope and I dined at Coudekerque with Jones and Barker — a full-out evening, a bit too much so for me!

19 & 20 September

A hurricane all yesterday for which I was devoutly thankful after the last night's dissipation. A very strong wind and low clouds all the morning of the 20th. Le Mesurier tested the air after lunch and almost stood still against the wind and was in clouds at 2,000ft. He reported conditions impossible, but despite this HQ insisted on our pushing off to Sparapellhoek and eleven of us left in two formations at 3.45 pm. We attained 10,000ft before we reached Fort Mardycke and, on turning, were over the Lines within five minutes of leaving Dunkirk. Dropped our bombs as nearly as possible over the target which, however, was never properly sighted as heavy clouds were over most of Belgium and travelling very rapidly. A tremendous fight back against the wind but fortunately AA not plentiful on account of the clouds and no EA seen — much too rough for them I guess. The wind was over 60mph at 14,000ft. The RFC escort thought we were quite mad to go under such conditions, but apparently a push is on and we may expect to have to raid in any conditions. Ten of us rushed off to a very good concert at La Panne immediately we got down and thus missed both tea and dinner, and ate far too much when we got back at 9.30 pm to ensure a peaceful night.

21 September

Up at 6 am for a raid on Sparapellhoek but did not take off till 7.45 am. Le Mesurier led the front formation and Jope the second, myself deputy leader on his left. Wind stronger than ever up top. Good formation going and we got a good line over the target, Sambrook scoring a direct hit on a hangar. Our formation good on the way back, but too high above Le M's and the escort too high above us. Umpteen EA encountered and many scraps, one Biff being shot down. Playford was shot through the hand and landed at the Frontier aerodrome with a badly shattered hand. Le Mesurier, Sproatt and Wright were also attacked but our formation was left alone. On the way home we fired hundreds of rounds into the trenches. I left in the touring car at 11 am to fly back Playford's bus, Jope and Dickson coming for a joy ride and Potts to examine the engine. DH, N5977 pretty badly shot up but fit to fly. We had lunch at the aerodrome. The CO, Mulock, was very nice and I got his permission to fly the German DFW Aviatik which had been brought down by A Flight of 3 Squadron. I found her an uncomfortable craft to fly, almost uncontrollable in bumps, there being little lateral control − small ailerons on the top plane only, inadequate for a good-sized two-seater. The 190hp Benz engine, however, is very nice to handle. Performance not impressive but has a good gliding angle and lands quite slowly. The DH was not ready till 6.30 pm and the engine was rather erratic, but I got her back all right. HQ wanted us to push off on another raid this afternoon but too many of our aircraft are out of action.

23 September

After a thoroughly dud day yesterday, conditions are still pretty rotten, nevertheless ten of us pushed off at 10.35 am for Varssenaere aerodrome, Le Mesurier leading. At just over 10,000ft we ran into thick misty cloud which overcast the whole sky and it was impossible to see even the next machine ahead. We flew just below it to Furnes where we picked up the Camel escort. They had just broken up and were diving down, so Le M, diving down steeply, gave the washout signal. I crossed the Lines and we dropped our bombs some four or five miles the other side, but thick clouds prevented observation. Le M and Jope followed us over and the three of us returned in formation. We then spent fifteen minutes diving down over the trenches and firing into the enemy positions. Landed at 12.15 pm. Sproatt, Omerod and Wright awarded DSCs. That makes nine, including the CO, and we now total more decorations in 5 Squadron than in any other squadron in the Dunkirk command. The Leugenboom gun pumped a few more 15in shells into Dunkirk, where they now have the 'take cover' procedure well taped. An observer on top of the cathedral tower notes the flash of the gun, which is clearly visible even in daylight. 'Mournful Mary' then sounds, and that gives people 1½ minutes to get under cover.

24 September

Ten of us led by Le Mesurier left at 10.45 am for Varssenaere. Good formation and picked up escort of eight Camels over Furnes at 13,000ft. Very heavy and accurate AA before we reached, and over, the target, a number of shells − both HE and shrapnel − bursting right amongst us. We got a very good line over the target and Sambrook scored two direct hits on hangars and several others very near. Bombs from other aircraft were seen to burst among the hangars and aircraft drawn up outside. Everybody seems to have made good shooting and an immense amount of damage must have been done. Formation was picked up quickly and well maintained, the escort too being excellent. On our return we fired many rounds into the enemy trenches. Nearly every one of our ten aircraft was hit, our left lower plane and propeller being holed. The AA was about as uncomfortably close as possible.

Jope, Sproatt, Gamon and Lupton, the latter two recent arrivals in the squadron, and myself went to the Malo cinema at 6 pm – rotten show. Whilst waiting for our car 'Mournful Mary' and all the other sirens started to scream and a moment later the air was alive with bursting shells. After ten minutes a car turned up and we made all speed to get to a healthier locality. Just as we passed through the Place de République two enormous explosions followed by a huge red glare took place in the direction of St Pol and the docks. Bombs were raining down and there was a huge blaze at the Depot where a direct hit with a large bomb wrecked the engine and repair shops. Both were entirely gutted and some 200 rotaries (Clergets, Le Rhones and ARs) destroyed, as well as all the lathes and other machinery. Certainly a warm day in more senses than one.

25 September
Eleven of us, led by Le Mesurier, took off at 11 am for Sparapellhoek aerodrome. Very good formation again, but RFC escort of Bristols would keep miles too high, some 4,000ft above us, which of course was useless. Good results and formation picked up well after dropping, which was as well as a formation of nine V–Strutter Albatros scouts came up from Thourout. However, they did not close with us, evidently considering our close formation too formidable. On the way back we spent some time patrolling up and down over the floods, blazing into the enemy trenches. We noticed many ruined farms and hamlets right in the heart of the flooded area. Flew low over the Depot before landing to have a close look at the damage. Playford came over in the afternoon. He leaves for England tomorrow and will probably not have the use of his hand for two months or more – so prospect of a good leave for him.

Jope and I went down to the Depot after tea. Two shops are utterly gutted and hundreds of engines of all sorts completely destroyed and partially melted. The repair shop which was magnificently equipped is entirely destroyed. Poor old Warwick Wright will have a job on his hands. It was a priceless moonlight night so Jope and I walked back. Enemy aircraft arrived overhead at 8 pm until about 10 pm, dropping many bombs. The searchlights picked up a Gotha and held it for about

90 seconds as it streaked out to sea heavily shelled. At 9.30 pm the Leugenboom gun opened up, dropping shells over with clockwork precision every seven minutes. The concussion tonight seemed heavier than usual and the whole place shook and reverberated for some seconds after each explosion. We watched the gunfire for some five or six rounds, the flash being distinctly seen in the sky away to the east although the gun is 27½ miles distant. Immediately the flash appeared all the warnings sounded and about 1 minute 40 seconds later the shell landed, and 17 seconds after that the noise of the gun firing reached us. She ceased firing at 11.30 pm for which we were thankful as we have to turn out tomorrow morning at 5.30 am.

26 September
Hauled out at 5.40 am for raid but conditions hopeless, clouds at 1,000ft completely overcasting the sky. Very disgruntled at being unnecessarily roused, we turned in again at 6.15 am. Low clouds all day. Hamilton and Blair came over to dinner, also Baker and the CO of 48 Squadron, RFC, to talk over tomorrow's raid on St Denis Westrem aerodrome.

> In the next few weeks 5 Naval were diverted from the Ypres battle, and ten raids were directed on one of the two main bases for the Gotha night bombers raiding S. E. England, at St Denis Westrem near Ghent. The Gotha's earlier daylight raids had caused quite negligible damage and loss of life but there had been panic and public squealing, forcing the Government to switch whole squadrons from the battlefront. Although the Gotha striking force was so small, it succeeded in drawing away huge resources for home defence; 376 aircraft; balloon, searchlight and AA units, the latter using up vast quantities of 3 inch shells in barrage fire. Airfields had to be constructed, and the output of factories over much larger areas was reduced as people took shelter.

27 September
Eleven of us left at 10.55 am for St Denis. Picked up our escort of five Biffs at 5,000 over Dunkirk and headed well out to sea. When at 9,000 off Nieuport Lupton got into a spin and lost 2,000ft but very gamely carried on, eventually catching up his position again by the time we turned in over Holland at 13,000ft. Wright and Mason turned back off Ostend with engine troubles. Clouds inland but many gaps and we picked up our target easily at 12.15, some very good work being put in. Sambrook got one of our 16lb through a Bessoneau hangar and dropped both 65lb amongst a group of eight Gothas on the aerodrome, which

must have been heavily damaged if not destroyed. Jackson, Le Mesurier's gunlayer, also obtained two direct hits on hangars and the remainder of his bombs fell amongst another group of Gothas. Many more hits claimed by other machines. We returned the way we came and the formation was perfect both ways, the escort too being good. Landed at 1.45 pm. Tennis after tea.

28 September

Heavy cloud masses early so raid postponed till 1 pm when, conditions having improved, eleven of us, led by Clarke, left for St Denis. RFC escort never turned up and, as we wasted some time waiting for them, Clarke rightly decided St Denis would run our petrol supply too fine and so we attacked Houttave instead. We got a good run over the sheds but Sambrook unfortunately dropped short. No direct hits observed. AA very heavy and accurate from Blankenberghe − a large burst just off our wing tip and another plumb underneath which threw us up bodily. A very thick haze made visibility indifferent and there were thick cloud masses inland. Three of our aircraft turned back with engine troubles. One solitary aircraft over at 9 pm and dropped about a dozen bombs.

29 September

Weather conditions again delayed operations until 2.15 pm. Then eleven of us, led by Clarke, left for St Denis Westrem. RFC escort picked up and we followed the coast well out to sea as far as Flushing which we skirted at 15,000ft, heading direct for Ghent which we reached, apparently unobserved, at 3.40 pm. I got a very good line over the target and Sambrook put three 16lb amongst a group of four Gothas, one 16lb and one 65lb on each side and very close up to an enormous six-engined aircraft which must have been heavily damaged, and another 16lb through the roof of a Bessoneau from which smoke poured. We must have damaged several Gothas with our bombs and many other machines scored hits on hangars and Bessoneaux, so altogether a pretty successful raid. Picked up formation heading for the coast. Our two rear aircraft were attacked by five Albatros scouts which, however, wouldn't close near enough for effective shooting. AA from Knocke very accurate until some six miles out to sea. On passing Nieuport I shut off and dived at 180mph, dropping from 15,000 to 12,000ft in eighteen seconds in a nearly vertical dive. Curious going down at that rate to see objects on the ground rapidly growing in size. Interesting views of the trenches and floods from 3,000ft. Landed at 5.6 pm. Very vigorous air offensive by the enemy from 8 to 10.30 pm, in the light of a full moon. Many very heavy bombs dropped and an enormous blaze in Dunkirk, which lit up the whole district with huge volumes of smoke obscuring a large part of the sky. One Gotha was held in the searchlights for two or three minutes but most AA was wide and low. The French gunners seem very ineffective compared with the Germans. Altogether about the most violent night we have had so far. Coudekerque's Handley Pages were in the air at the same time, returning at about 10.45 pm.

The six-engined aircraft was undoubtedly one of the Staaken 'Giants' of which only 18 were built. With a 2 ton load and crew of seven they could just manage 80mph. However, flying at 10,000-16,000ft, fighters never reached them when they made solo raids on London and half were lost in crashes.

30 September

A lovely day but a stand-off for us after a strenuous week, and in order to get our engines teed up. Six raids last week. I must put in a word here for the very fine work of our fitters, riggers and armourers who are putting up a marvellous show, as they always do, and we have a fine lot of gunlayers who keep their Lewises and our front Vickers in perfect trim. We don't get many opportunities of using our front guns except for trench strafing, and that is unofficial. In close formation, in the event of attack, the rear gunner does the shooting, with the pilot concentrating on keeping station and giving the gunner as far as possible the best angle of fire, only using his front guns on anything more or less directly ahead. But the Hun invariably attacks from astern or abeam, usually diving down steeply.

After breakfast we went to see where a fairly large bomb had burst in the farmyard on the canal bank some 300 yards away. It being Sunday, there was a short service at 10.30. An enemy photographic bus came over at 12.45 pm, clearly visible in the sunlight at about 18,000ft. AA heavy but thousands of feet too low — one wonders whether their guns are able to reach that height? Went into Dunkirk at 4.30 to view last night's damage. Very extensive. Heavy damage in Jean Bart's Square and all down the Rue de l'Église. A 'heavy' exploded just in front of the cathedral tower, more or less wiping out the Tavern Charles and neighbouring buildings and completely wrecking an RFC car, killing the driver and two RFC officers. Another burst by the Tavern Jules did extensive damage, but by far the worst damage was caused where some dozen bombs in quite a small radius in one of the poorer quarters by the water towers completely demolished many houses. This was the enormous blaze, which occurred in a brewery. Nearly every street was a shambles. A 'heavy' burst in the station square and another by the railway crossing near Petite Synthe. Total casualties amounted to 125. Several 600lb bombs reported to have been dropped. Graham of Seaplanes went up after them on a Pup and had an engagement with a Gotha, apparently killing their gunner and outing one of their engines, but with his gun jamming he had to break off. We hear rumours of four DSOs being recommended for the last St Denis raid, but I don't think there is much chance of any coming through – the Admiralty are jealous of their youngest Service stealing the thunder!

1 October

Another priceless day. Eight of us, led by Clarke, left at 11.30 for St Denis. Jope dropped out early with a broken con rod. Escort picked up over Dunkirk and, heading well out to sea, turned in as usual just short of Flushing at 15,000, arriving over the target at 1 pm, observing as we approached that a large hangar had been burnt to the ground – a result of last night's Handley Page expedition. Getting a good line from west-south-west to east-north-east, we again got excellent results, Sambrook putting one 16lb right on top of a Gotha in the middle of a line of four and also direct hits with both 65lb on a tent and a Bessoneau from which smoke and flames issued. St John also got a direct hit on a Bessoneau and several other hits were reported. Altogether a very successful outing. Formation and escort were good. Several EA came up after us when off Zeebrugge on return but were attacked by Camels and two driven down in spins. Reached 18,000ft on the way home. Enemy aircraft over as usual between 9.30 pm and midnight. I turned in, however, at 10 pm, preferring bed to the dugout, and slept through most of it. I was promoted to Flight Lieutenant with effect from 1 October, 1917.

2 October

Heavy damage done last night at the Depot and St Pol. At the former a large hangar was burnt out and the sides of several others blown out. A bomb dropped on the Le Pecq bomb store scattered several over the countryside, a number being picked up in the village of St Pol. On the St Pol aerodrome two French Bessoneaux were gutted and ten Voisins destroyed, and one of 2 Squadron's Bessoneaux burnt out complete with three DH4s. Seven of us, led by Clarke, left at 12.30 pm for St Denis. Escort picked up over Dunkirk and the objective reached, by the usual course, at 2 pm. Good results again obtained, Sambrook placing a 65lb in the middle of a group of Gothas and the other between the group and a Bessoneau some 20yds away – both must have inflicted heavy damage.

One or two other hits reported. AA heavy and accurate, two HE bursts alongside as we made our run across the target. Only the leader of the escort with us on the return journey. We had to fight back against a strong wind and did not land until 3.30 pm. My 14th raid in the last eighteen days and 10th on St Denis, the last four being about the most successful Sambrook and I have carried out. So far as observations can tell, direct hits were obtained on Gothas or Bessoneaux on each one.

3 October

At last the weather has broken and given us all a not unwelcome rest. I went into town after tea and walked out to the Depot, being picked up on the way by Jope and St John on Douglases. The damage at the Depot is colossal — one large and one small hangar utterly destroyed and all the other hangars perforated and their sides blown out. The small arms store wrecked and an enormous crater filling the site of the former bomb store. I ran into Whaley who tells me some 200 bombs were dropped on the Depot on the night of 1 October and, in all, 200 engines and 150 aircraft destroyed, including some at St Pol aerodrome. The Depot is being disbanded.

4 October

Heavy rain and wind all day. I saw Warwick Wright for a few minutes and he puts the damage done on the night of 1 October at seven millions — sounds a high estimate to me, but he should know. Many guests to dinner.

5 October

Heavy rain and wind kept us grounded. Jope and I went into town at 6 pm and dined with Sieveking. In the middle of dinner a very violent and sudden clap of thunder sent several more or less terror-stricken people scuttling for the cellars — it certainly sounded and shook the place like a fairly large bomb.

11 October

After a week of heavy rain, thunderstorms and strong winds, conditions improving and, though still a fairly strong north wind and heavy masses of cumulus, a few gaps enable A and C Flights to push off on a raid at 11.45 am. They returned at 1.30 pm, having visited Sparapellhoek with fairly good results. Most of us went to an exceptionally good concert at the Malo Casino. Oswald Rae of Harry Tate's Company was screamingly funny in a number of turns, including Harry Tate in 'Motoring'. Also two very good singers and a really first class conjurer.

12 October
Standing by all day for a raid, but weather impossible. A rough-house in the Ward Room at 10 pm resulting in much damage which will no doubt be charged up on our mess bills. Le Mesurier went quite mad, bust all the globes, overturned the table, smashed glasses and hurled chairs about, finishing with a grand mêlée in the dark with Jope and I.

14 October
Sunday. John Gamon went on leave. A bright and sunny day but the aerodrome being more or less under water after two days of incessant rain, flying quite impossible. A great crowd in Goberts for tea, after which Omerod, Shaw and I walked out to Malo and along the sands to look for a French 1½ Strutter which had landed on the beach. While waiting for the squadron tender at the Arcades, 'Mournful Mary' and all the other sirens in the town awoke the echoes and, with bombs falling and much AA overhead, we made haste to leave, passing on our way the jute factory blazing furiously from a direct hit. Five minutes after getting back, while sitting in the Mess, six bombs burst with terrific force very close. The Mess hut fairly rocked and we all dived under the tables as each detonation seemed nearer than the last. We were just recovering when down we all went again as five more burst nearer still. Never before experienced such stunning concussions. Only about a dozen of us sat down to dinner at 7.30, the rest having repaired to the dugout and only turning up some twenty minutes later when all was quiet and retiring to their refuge after a very hurried repast. Later Pownall, Dickson and I with the aid of torches proceeded to dig for fuses in the numerous craters, finding one. The bombs appear to have been only 26lb but being fused for contact made more noise than the 185lb delayed action bombs dropped on a former occasion.

15 October
Rain in the early morning but cleared after breakfast and, despite a semi-waterlogged aerodrome and inches of mud, ten of us pushed off at 12.30 for Varssenaere. I was fully prepared to hit the ditch at 50 knots and do a somersault into the next field, but somehow we got away all right without even a splintered propeller. Jope turned back with pressure trouble and Cleghorn later, being unable to maintain height or speed. We struck enormous cumulus masses at 6,000ft which towered up to a tremendous height above us. Escort of five Biffs picked up at 14,000 and we crossed the Lines near Dixmude. At 15,000 the huge cloud formations were still towering high above us and casting such deep shadows that much of the country below was obscured. Fortunately,

1. The author in 1917.

2. The Bristol Scout advanced trainer, "a handy little aircraft with an 80hp engine" (p.6).

3. Cockpit of a Bristol Scout – the "office".

4. Henri Farman 27 two-seater bomber. The type of aircraft in which the author began his training.

5. The author in a Sopwith 1½ strutter (see p. 10).

6. Nieuport two-seater fighter at Coudekerque.

7. "One Triplane touched down in the wheat and turned a somersault" (p.63).

8. Sopwith Pup "Julia" piloted by Flight Sub-Lieutenant "Ally" Shaw.
   It's flying qualities were described as, "impeccable — as light as a
   feather".

9. 205 Squadron's Lancia tender ends in the ditch on a run ashore.

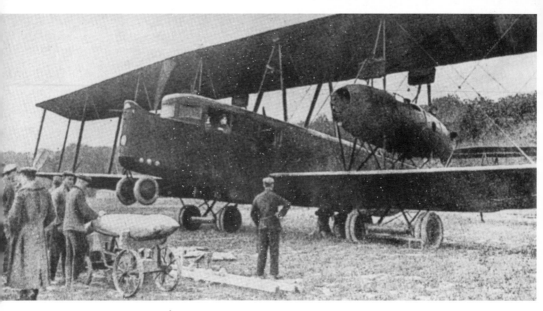

10. Four-engined Staaken RV1 "Giant" preparing to bomb London, 1917 (see p.85). (*Imperial War Museum*)

11. British 15″ gun monitor HMS *Marshal Ney* off Zeebrugge. (*Imperial War Museum*)

12. The French fighter ace, Charles Nungesser, in front of his Nieuport Scout, which was emblazoned with the device of skull and cross-bones, coffin and candlesticks. He was credited with 45 kills (see p.44).

13. 1½ strutter after a crash.

14. "Sands landed a large Short on the CO's office at Coudekerque this morning, ripping off the roof and completely wrecking the machine. The CO was fortunately out" (p.44).

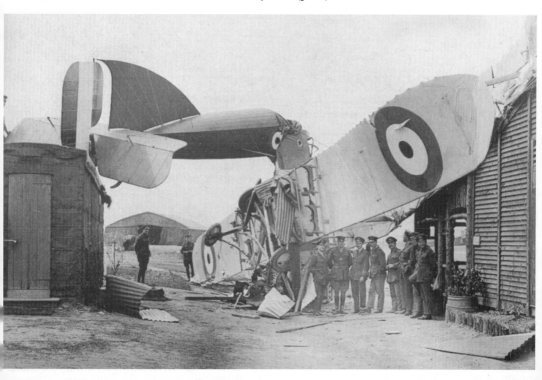

15. "The first Handley Page arrived from Manston" (p.34).

16. "Went to the Depot to examine a captured Albatros scout" (p.60).

17. "Gardener brought over the first 200hp Hispano Sopwith B1 for testing"(p.47).

18. Sub-Lieutenant Sproatt with Bristol Scout.

19. DH4 in which the author flew 35 missions. "They handled well
    and the Rolls Eagle VI proved wonderfully reliable" (p.58).

20. The author about to take Colonel Dugdale (USA) up in his DH4.

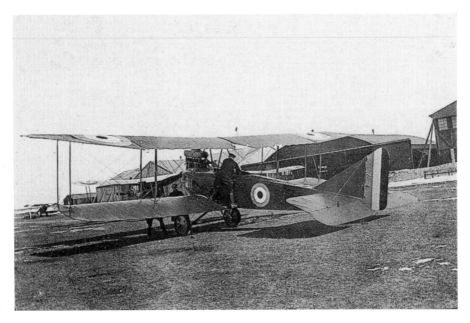

21. "I got permission to fly the German DFW Aviatik which had been brought down by A Flight of B Squadron" (p.81).

22. Bleriot XI Trainer at Eastchurch.

23. Twin-Anzani-engined Caudron bomber which carried a bomb aimer or observer as well as the pilot (see p. 10).

24. DH4s about to leave on a raid from Petit Synthe.

25. The Bristol "Bullet" was one of the most unlucky aeroplanes of the First World War, being condemned to virtual obscurity owing to prejudice against monoplanes. It was fast, and, the author says in his log book, "quite comfortable".

26. Jope-Slade, the author's best friend, demonstrating DH4's guns.

27. "Newton-Clare had a bad crash on N5114 with Warwick Wright as passenger" (p.33).

28. Sopwith 1½ strutter, showing the unusual interplane strutting from which the aircraft's name was derived. This is the two-seater version, night bombing being undertaken by the single-seater.

29. Ready for take-off from Coudekerque in winter.

30. The French 'Cannon' Voisin (see p.34).

Varssenaere was in the clear and we were able to get a good line across it with some effective work being done. AA very heavy and pretty accurate, the air 2–300ft above us being literally full of shrapnel puffs and the HE more or less on our level. Several of us got holed but nothing serious. Our escort, for reasons best known to themselves, chose to return overland getting very heavily shelled all the way back to the Lines which served them jolly well right. Off Ostend, on our return, an enormous cumulus cloud towered up to fully 18,000ft, giving us healthy bumps from fully half a mile away. I've never seen such high cumulus formations before. Exceedingly cold up today, we all suffered from it, and a Sidcot suit, flying helmet and gauntlets only are not much protection at 15,000ft in an open cockpit.

Extract from letter to his mother dated 17 October, 1917
'...not been much doing lately on account of the weather, but the day before yesterday relieved the monotony with a stunt (my 50th). We have also had one or two lively nights but for the most part rain and high winds are the order of the day. I wish we could have a few weeks dry weather for the sake of our push — if only we could get the whole of the Ridge and Houthoult Forest events would march pretty quickly I think. It would be nice to see the Hun evacuating Belgium [but this push ended in Passchendaele].

Russia looks to be in rather a serious position again, but events that side are not really of great consequence. I think the signs of mutiny in the German Navy are encouraging. I think the Hun forces, Naval and Military, are getting very fed up and disheartened and rapidly declining in fighting value.

It was tremendously cold flying on Monday and nearly everybody complained of a touch of frostbite somewhere; we shall have to wrap up more thoroughly and grease our faces well in future.'

18 October
After two days of very strong winds, a sunny morning with again large cumulus formations. Ten of us left at 10.40 am for Varssenaere, picking up our Biff escort over Furnes and crossing the Lines at 14,000. Clear view of the target through cloud gaps and a good run over it, but Wilkinson, my gunlayer in Sambrook's absence, could not observe results, though he thinks our bombs fell among the hangars — they should have done on the line we steered. AA on return was extremely heavy and accurate and, in spite of violent switchbacking and side-slipping, pretty well every machine was hit. Le Mesurier who for fun escorted us in a Triplane (A Flight standing off) got hit through the

cowl and landed at 48 Squadron. On crossing the Lines I dived down repeatedly over the German trenches, blazing away with my front gun, and finally flew up and down the floods near Nieuport, but nobody seemed to take much notice. Priceless view of the trench system and the flooded area. Nieuport looks nearly levelled now, many shells bursting in the canals. Our escort claim to have downed a Hun over Dixmude.

19 October

Awakened at 12.30 am by a very heavy destroyer bombardment. Some 300 or more shells were put over in the course of ten minutes, the landscape being brilliantly lit up by a number of very powerful star shells. One distinctly heard the scream of shells overhead and it was not surprising to find in the morning a dozen or more craters on and just off the boundaries of the aerodrome. Old man Hun is evidently bent on causing us as much damage and annoyance as possible, but he has not had much luck so far. We, however, are not the only target. A very dud day with low clouds.

20 October

Bright sunny day for a change but very hazy. Eight of us left at 10.35 am for a new target, Engel aerodrome, some three miles west of Aertrycke. Picked up our escort at 13,000 over Furnes and approached our target at 14,000, but very difficult to spot it until almost overhead on account of the thick haze and a small cloud completely covering the aerodrome. I, however, saw the village of Engel and the ammunition dump clearly and from that knew exactly where to look and could distinguish one white Bessoneau just off the edge of the cloud, and by the time I reached it the cloud had obligingly moved off. Our bombs fell amongst buildings in the north corner of the aerodrome which look exactly like hangars, but aren't. Several others also bombed them. No doubt they were full of stores and worth destroying. AA heavy but inaccurate, the thick haze evidently preventing them seeing us clearly. Spent some time on the way home diving on Hun trenches but could not get my gun to work properly. No tea today as, in future, we are having dinner at 5.30 pm to enable the 'windy' ones to have their meal before rushing for the dugout! Personally, I feel if one is going to be hit one will be hit and why suffer discomfort – a direct hit on the dugout would wipe out the lot anyway. A Secret Service report through on the results of the St Denis Westrem raids: '...large hangar and twelve Bessoneaux completely destroyed, wireless station destroyed, at least five Gothas destroyed, many others damaged...' Intermittent EA visits from 6.30 to 8.30 pm. Several heavy bombs dropped over Coudekerque way. The monitor *Terror* was damaged and driven ashore in the destroyer bombardment on the night of 19 October. From accounts, a destroyer got within 800yds of her and emptied a broadside into her and capped that with a torpedo before she had time to know what was happening.

21 October

It should have been B Flight's stand-off and I lay abed thinking to indulge until 11 am but had to tumble out at 9.30 as all serviceable aircraft are going. Ten of us took off at 11 am, led by Clarke, for Houttave and Vlisseghem aerodromes. Five Biffs picked up at 13,000 over La Panne and we headed out to sea. Observed monitors, escorted by destroyers, bombarding Ostend from off Nieuport. On turning in over the coast just west of Wenduyne we saw a formation of six EA fighters pass 1,500ft below us heading in the opposite direction, also several more high up over Blankenberghe, so we knew what to expect before we got away again!

Vlisseghem showed up clearly and we managed to get a good line from north-west to south-east but my gunlayer, Wilkinson, was too perturbed by the numbers of Huns sculling around to steer me dead on and our bombs exploded on the aerodrome some 80yds in front of the row of hangars. However, that was nearer than most of the others got, bombs being scattered broadcast as the Huns closed in on us. Immediately after dropping I saw an Albatros attacking my next DH ahead. I got my sights on him and he should have been a 'sitter' but my front gun jammed hopelessly due to a broken belt. Wilkinson let him have a tray as he swung round and he sheered off towards the rear of our formation. Meanwhile numerous running fights were going on. Altogether there were about a dozen Huns, maybe more, but in the general mix-up it was difficult to see. Le Mesurier was shot up badly by two EA that attacked him, a longeron being nearly severed by an explosive bullet, also main spar and oil pipe shot through and 37 holes in his machine — one bullet tearing through his Sidcot suit at the knee without as much as grazing him. We counted seven holes in N6004 on getting down, but some of these were from HE, several bursts getting very near as we came out over Blankenberghe. Practically all our aircraft were hit. Shaw's gunlayer shot one attacker down out of control and Sproatt drove another down in a vertical dive. Our escort sat 2,000ft above us all this time making no attempt to come down to our assistance. On the way back, however, they had several scraps over Ostend, driving an Albatros down in a spin and shooting down a two-seater in flames. Altogether quite an interesting morning. Baker and Dixon of 48

Squadron came over on a Biff at 3.30 and we yarned over the morning's excitements. The usual old Belgian Maurice Henry★ came over our drome low down at 10.30 and immediately turned round and made off towards the Lines, no doubt with news that we were about to leave on a raid. I'd love to shoot the beast down. I'm sure he gives us away every time. They are a nation of spies.

Great controversy in the evening over the dinnertime question and, on being put to the ballot, the 'windy brigade' secured a majority, so I suppose dinner will continue at the absurd time of 5.30 pm. On the night of the 20th a 500 kilo bomb fell alongside a Bessoneau at St Pol making a crater 37ft across and 20ft deep. The Bessoneau largely disappeared and its contents of Camels and DH4s were disintegrated. I lay abed feeling rather dud, the weather also being dud. I turned out at 9.30, however, as B Flight was again down for a raid at 12.30. Several of our aircraft being out of action, A and C Flights only went, taking off for St Denis at 12.30. They returned at 2.30 pm having bombed the Zeebrugge Mole, heavy cloud and bad visibility preventing them reaching Ghent. I took Holloway, from the Chinks' camp, up in N5993 at 3.45 pm. We went up to Nieuport and I flew over the remains of the town and the floods at 2,000ft, firing two good bursts into the German trenches till they started shelling us with small HE and getting a few quite close — quite an enterprise for Holloway who had never been in the air before. Very large numbers of our own kite balloons up and our artillery appeared to be pretty active.

24 October
Dull early but cleared by 10 am, though very strong wind. RFC pilot brought over a 375hp DH4 for 2 Squadron. It has an extraordinary climb and is very fast. I wish we were getting them — just 100hp more than our DHs. Le Mesurier left on a month's leave. He is nervously strung up and needs it. Tested N5978 at 3.40 pm. Her new engine doesn't get her up anything like as well as the old one — ten minutes to 7,000ft unladen. Unpleasant up — thick mist at just over 6,000 and very bumpy.

26 October
We experienced a hurricane most of yesterday but today is a Z day and a raid planned for 6.30 am, a second one to follow later, but the weather is thoroughly dud so nothing doing. I returned at 4.30 pm from a visit to Dunkirk to find that Dickson and Lupton, much to

★ A Farman 2-seater pusher biplane.

everyone's surprise, had been pushed off on their own to Thourout on a stunt in very poor weather conditions — completely overcast sky with storms and squalls about and a strong wind. Apparently the Wing Commander had rung up asking for two pilots to volunteer to go and the CO averse to it, had given Lupton and Dickson the opportunity, which of course was accepted, without calling for volunteers from the whole squadron. In fact no one knew anything about it until after the two had left, and there was much feeling of discontent about it. The squadron have always worked as a team and there is a feeling that this sort of thing may disrupt its smooth running. As a matter of fact the weather conditions were most unsuitable, as the CO had undoubtedly stressed, and as time was short and it would soon be dusk, I fancy he had to make a quick decision. Dickson got back at 5.20 when it was just dusk, having caught glimpses of Thourout but been unable to observe any results and been badly strafed by AA. Lupton got lost in the clouds and eventually found he had been drifted by the strong west wind right away over Bruges. He was lucky to get back at all and pulled off a good bit of work by landing in the dark at 5.45 by the aid of searchlights and flares. EA over again between 12.30 and 2 am.

27 October

A day of grievous internal troubles. Jope apparently overstepped the mark last night and told the CO off in very strong terms about the Thourout affair. The Wing Commander has taken the matter to Wing Captain Lambe who may order a court martial, so things look serious for poor old Jope, who is in the meantime transferred to 2 Squadron and loses his acting rank. As a result of all this and a certain amount of friction that has existed between the senior officers and the CO, Clarke and St John leave for England tomorrow, Garrett goes to Wing HQ and Wally Newton Clare to the Depot. Sproatt, myself and Omerod take over A, B and C Flights respectively and are given the rank of acting Flight Commander. What momentous changes, hardly any of the old original crowd left, only Sproatt and myself left of the early Coudekerque days. I'm awfully sorry for poor old Jope, but I was afraid something would happen. He is inclined to be hasty and outspoken but is an awfully good fellow. Eight of us left at 1.20 pm for Sparapellhoek, led by Sproatt. Quite a good raid, though clouds made observation difficult. AA very accurate and intense, we collected three large rips through our tail and most of the DHs were hit. Some ten to fifteen EA in two formations followed us back to the Lines, but didn't close on us because our formation was very tight. Sambrook has been passed by the selection committee for training as a pilot and I now have Le Mesurier's old gunlayer, Jackson. He is excellent and flies quite well but unfortunately for me he too soon goes before the selection committee. Our strafed tail prevented any stunting over the floods.

8

A Visit to the Palace

Despite the upheavals of the last few days, the squadron is determined to carry on the traditions of the past and, with the types of pilots coming through recently, especially such men as Lupton and Gamon, the standard will be fully maintained. I think we all now feel that the CO had to act as he did. There was no time for consultations and anyway several of us were off the station at the time — besides, what is a CO for if not to take firm decisions on his own?

28 October
Clarke and St John left for England at 8.40 am. Six of us left at 10.50 am for Varssenaere, myself leading on DH, N6000. Formation very good and we picked up our Biff escort dead on time at 11.45 am over Bray Dunes. Clouds thick over the Lines and I expected some difficulty in spotting the target, but I picked up Ghistelles spire and then the aerodrome through a gap and so steered on for Jabbeke where a large clear gap enabled us to get a good view of our target. We loosed off on a good line from south to north over the eastern hangars and Jackson obtained a direct hit with a 65lb on a hangar. Three Gothas were on the aerodrome. The formation picked up very quickly on me and the escort were A1. A very nasty shelling all the way home and we got the closest shave I've ever had from AA, a shell (luckily not a large one) bursting with a violent crash 20ft plumb underneath us and tearing a huge hole in the fuselage just in front of the back seat. I could feel the concussion right through my feet and up my legs. Fortunately Jackson was not touched but he nearly fell through the hole! Had the shell been one of the larger variety we should undoubtedly have fallen in pieces, but it couldn't have been larger than a 3in. Many others were also close. Some seven or eight EA well below us close to the floods were scrapping with our Camels and we saw two go down out of control. Shut off over the floods and dived, blazing away with both front guns at the Hun trenches. Several fair-sized bursts of HE alongside so did not stay for more.

Newton Clare left in the afternoon. Squadron Commander Allsop turned up at about 4 pm and the CO being off the station and Sproatt in the air, I entertained him but he didn't stay long. AA very heavy and incessant and enemy aircraft violent again in the evening. Many bombs dropped fairly near, three falling on Coudekerque, one within ten yards of 7A Squadron's Mess, but did no more damage than blowing out all the windows. Sproatt, Omerod and myself promoted to acting Flight Commanders.

29 October

The CO away all day so we ran the squadron on our own. Stood by for a raid until 2 pm when it was finally washed out on account of thick clouds and a strong west wind. I took N5974 up for a test flight at 2.30 pm with Lupton in the back. Not at all nice on the controls and did her best to spin when I put her into a steep spiral. Landed at St Pol and saw Jope for a few minutes. Gale forecast but it cleared nevertheless and was a lovely moonlight evening with sheets of mackerel sky high up. Enemy aircraft over between 8 and 10.30 pm but they confined their attention mostly to Bergues and Audryckes localities. We saw two Gothas very distinctly against the mackerel clouds, also numbers of Camels, Nieuports and Handley Pages were up.

30 October

Deluges of rain all the morning and afternoon, as usual on a Z Day when we had three raids planned − the first to start at 6.30 am, but none came off. I dined in town with Sieveking and Barker from 7 Squadron. Jope should have made a fourth but did not turn up. We also saw Rochford, Elwood and others. It had cleared to a fine night when we came out from dinner so we made haste to quit Dunkirk. The Huns dropped a very brilliant green starshell which lit up the country for miles around. Five minutes after getting back, while sitting in the Mess, six bombs burst with terrific force very close and the hut fairly rocked. We were all sprawling flat before the second burst and each one seemed nearer than the last. Within fifteen seconds we were again diving under tables as five more fell even closer.

31 October

Awakened at 3.30 am by the usual frightfulness which went on more or less violently until 5 am. AA very active and several large crumps from bombs fairly near, but didn't trouble to get up. I was acting CO all the morning and afternoon. Six of us left at 12.5 pm for Sparappelhoek. Escort picked up as usual and we crossed the lines just north of Dixmude. We got a few fairly close bursts of HE before reaching the target; there were also numbers of EA skulking around. A drifting cloud prevented observation of results but we dropped on a good line south-west to north-east. Those skulking EA closed with us just after we had crossed the target, but we bunched up close and, Jackson being in good form with both guns while I weaved the bus about, they found matters too hot and nothing approached within 100 yards, at which range many of our tracers were hitting them. Gamon got his tail shot about pretty badly. The escort, who were about 800ft above us, also let them have it. Usual visitors between 9 and 11 pm and AA heavy.

1 November
A dull day and heavy drizzle at 2.30 pm. Our visitor, Colonel Moorshead, was keen to be taken up despite the weather conditions and the CO handed him over to me. After an official photo had been taken in front of the plane, with a group of us standing in front, we took off in DH4, N6000 at 1.40 pm. Thick mist at 1,000ft and I climbed steadily trying to get through it, but at 3,500ft it was as thick as ever and, my compass showing different bearings, I shut off and on coming through discovered myself over Malo. Continued along the coast at 800ft as far as Nieuport, circling for a time just over the outskirts of the town, giving the colonel a good view of its shattered condition. We then flew over the floods for some distance in the direction of Dixmude and Ypres before turning for home at a few hundred feet with conditions steadily deteriorating — heavy drizzle and Scotch mist as we landed. The colonel seemed to have enjoyed his flight despite the conditions, but I think disappointed that we were not shelled! I thought I ought not to risk a guest colonel. Tea at Goberts with Omerod and Jope. The court martial we hope may be quashed and Jope didn't have too bad a time with the Wing Commander yesterday.

4 November
After three very dud days it is at last sunny and almost cloudless and the wind round to the east — which is where we like it. Battling home against a strong west wind with plenty of EA about and accurate AA is no fun! A and C Flights left at 1 pm for Engel and returned at 2.45 pm having come in for a fair amount of scrapping. Mason's and Shaw's machines badly shot up and the latter's gunlayer, Burne, wounded in two places in the leg, but not seriously. He apparently shot one Albatros down as it fell out of control with its propeller stopped. The RFC escort also sent one down in flames. I took up N5992 for test at 3 pm with a new gunlayer, Foster. We spent half an hour patrolling the floods. Much activity seen, large numbers of our aircraft up, including an old twin-engined Caudron escorted by two Nieuports which kept crossing

the Lines to a point some four miles the other side and some three miles north-east of Dixmude, evidently on photographic reconnaissance.

6 November

Dull and threatening all day. Shaw and I did a tramp along the Cassel road, in the morning and got caught in the rain. Dined at Coudekerque with Sieveking and Jope, meeting also Brackley, Darley, Scott, Rose and others. They have a fine new Mess and Ward Room, a great improvement on our old single hut and separate Gun Room in the sleeping hut area. The Handleys left at 11 pm for Thourout — an impressive sight to see those huge monsters drone away into the night.

10 November

Weather bad again and non-duty watch taken for a route march in the morning. I, not feeling very good, stayed behind as CO. One or two Huns over in the evening — evidently after this place — and dropped some large ones just the other side of the canal. Sproatt, England and I sat up talking ghosts till midnight.

11 November

Still very unsettled after four days of impossible weather. Barker and Darley of Squadrons 7 and 7A are going over tomorrow to collect their DSCs at a special investiture — lucky beggars. We here cannot be spared! The Wing Commander came over yesterday and decorated our gunlayer Darby with a Distinguished Service Medal on Divisions at 1.30 pm. Dallas and Minifie from 1 (N) Squadron came over to dinner.

12 November

A sunny morning at last with sharp frost early. Aircraft on the tarmac at 9 am but the aerodrome being half under water and exceedingly sloppy everywhere, there was considerable doubt as to our chances of taking off with bombs. So I took up N5962 at 9.30 to try it out and got away with it all right, landing a few minutes later. RFC could not escort us, so eight of us left at 11.30 pm on our own — Omerod, Lupton, Gamon and Mason with bombs, Sproatt, Cleghorn, Dickson and myself as fighter escort. All took off all right but up to 4,000ft the haze was so thick one could barely see an aircraft 100 yards away, and couldn't see the ground at all except for white roads and the sand dunes. Omerod led the bombers right up to Calais before turning, apparently not realizing the strength of the east wind, which we battled against for an hour and a half to reach the area of our target, Vlisseghem, which he apparently failed to see as we watched it carefully and none of the bombers passed over it. AA was very heavy and accurate, Blankenberghe putting their first salvo bang on our level at 17,000ft which we had reached in our battle against the wind. Knowing our normal level was 14–15,000, that was pretty good rangefinding on their part. On turning we were immediately over Ostend and within five minutes across the Lines at Nieuport. We all suffered thick heads for the rest of the day due no doubt to that extra 2,000ft. Cleghorn crashed on landing, feeling dizzy and queer at the time, but no one hurt apart from the aircraft. A tremendous strafe going on all day in the Nieuport area, with firing heavy and incessant.

13 November

A fine day but very thick and foggy early. The heavy strafe continued all through the night and rumour has it that the Germans had taken Nieuport and were across the floods up that extreme northern end of the Lines — not very cheering if true. Two large German reconnaissance aircraft, escorted by four fighters, were overhead at a great height at 11 am. The French AA, as usual, well below them. We were down for a dawn stunt, Zeppelin-strafing, the German Fleet being out with escorting Zepps, but early fog prevented us taking off, and later on they had apparently run for home.

Eight of us, myself leading, took off at 1.30 pm for Houttave. RFC escort picked up as usual and we proceeded up the coast well out to sea. Noticed a large vessel being heavily shelled off Middlekerke, fountains of water going up all round her. Just before turning in over Wenduyne four EA passed 2,000ft below us flying in the opposite direction, and we fully expected to meet them on the way back, but, much to our joy, they apparently had other things to do. Our bombs released on a good line but the wind drifted us just too far south and they fell 50 yards from the line of hangars. AA very heavy and accurate, the sky being literally full of exploding shells of all sizes. This apparently accounted for several of our formation streaking out to sea without forming up on the leader. I purposely headed for the coast between Wenduyne and Ostend at a slow speed to enable our escort to form right up on us, but one or two others dashing out over Blankenberghe drew the rest with them and, of course, Blankenberghe gave them hell, which was only to be expected. Gamon stuck with me and we got comparatively little near us. I managed to cut in and assume the lead again off Ostend. The escort, with one exception, returned inland for reasons best known to themselves and got heavily strafed by Westende. Numbers of EA about, but none came to close quarters. Enemy aircraft over again in force from 6 pm onwards and a large number of bombs fell all round us, a few uncomfortably close to our huts.

15 November

Six of us, Omerod leading, left at 10.45 am for Uytkerke aerodrome. Escort picked up south of Furnes. A 60-70mph north wind at 15,000ft made progress so slow that after battling with it for 25 minutes we were still south of Furnes — so Uytkerke was out of the question. Omerod then decided to try for Sparapellhoek, but though he had such convincing evidence of the direction and strength of the wind, he failed utterly to allow for it and we were soon drifting over Dixmude. I tried several times to pull him round, heading my machine more into wind, but for a long time he failed to notice where we were drifting. When at last he did he wouldn't come round enough, with the result that we were over Houthulst Forest and the Passchendaele sector of the Lines, a good ten miles south of Dixmude and fifteen miles south of our course, before he headed fully into wind. It then took us thirty minutes fighting in the teeth of the wind before we reached Handzaeme where we dropped our loads, still seven miles south of our proper course, our petrol and tempers by this time being nearly exhausted. We eventually landed at 1.20 pm, having been up a full hour longer than the target warranted without ever getting within ten miles of it. I'm afraid I've now not much confidence in O as a leader, but he is a very good fellow and quite a good pilot. Conditions were certainly difficult. Had it not been for clouds one or two of us would almost certainly have been brought down by AA, as at a ground speed of about 30mph against that wind we were sitting targets. At times they put up a salvo very close and the next still closer when, luckily, they apparently lost us.

Cleghorn failed to return and was missing until 6.30 pm when we had word that his DH caught fire at 8,000ft, but by diving it at 220mph he managed to get down and land: both he and his gunlayer, Foster, being unhurt but his DH burned lustily on the ground before they could extinguish the fire. A court of enquiry was held at St Pol, preparatory to Jope's court martial which comes off tomorrow.

16 November

Weather pretty dud and proposed raid washed out as several of our numbers, not including myself fortunately, have to attend the court martial. I took Taffy Edwards, who was over from Vendôme to collect a Pup, up in N6000 and showed him Nieuport and the Lines, over which we flew at 2-3,000. Layers of mist and clouds at all heights from less than 1,000 up to 9-10,000 made flying not over-pleasant but we were up for 1½ hours nevertheless. I dived on the German trenches several times but could only get single-shot firing out of both guns, their muzzle attachments being off for cleaning purposes. Jope has come out of his court martial with nothing worse than a reprimand. His future is unlikely to be adversely affected, though of course he has lost his acting rank.

17 November

Another foggy and thoroughly dud day. Taffy Edwards and I went down to the Depot after lunch and watched a hockey match between 2 Squadron and 7 & 7A, the latter winning 3-2. I went up to the Mess and pulled Jope out and brought him along, hearing from him the full account of the court martial, which seems to have been very sympathetic towards him although of course they were bound to convict. He is already a great favourite at 2 Squadron where I stopped to tea and dinner − a nice and full-out crowd.

19 November

Overcast all day. I tested radiator blinds on N5974 at 11.30, taking Taffy Edwards with me. Thick clouds at 3,000 and not very enjoyable. Dickson crashed one of C Flight's best aircraft trying to land 20ft up on 48 Squadron's 'drome. Strong wind and a falling barometer doesn't promise well for tomorrow.

20 November

Impossible weather with hurricanes of wind has now hit us for a whole week, so nothing doing against our friends the enemy who have also let us alone. Most of 48 Squadron RFC came to dinner one evening and told us of the loss of one of their Biffs which was shot down in flames by six EA who dived out of the clouds at 2,000ft well our side of the Lines. The observer jumped from 1,500ft − no parachute! Two days ago I took up N5974 for a test and pushed through the thick cloud layer at 4,000ft into glorious sunshine, an incredible change after the gloom below − a few wisps of cirrus high above and a glistening sea of fleecy clouds below, with towering masses of cumulus on the horizon. The scene was so enchanting and such a change after the gloom of the past week that I decided to stay up and explore the clouds, but at 8,000ft the radiator cap blew off and a stream of hot water flying back into my face caused a hasty descent into the gloom again. Le Mesurier arrived from London on a 1½ Strutter to collect his gear, flying back at 3 pm. Nice to see him again. Several went over to St Omer for a joy ride and tea, but I decided, in the heavy tender and bitter cold, it was not good enough.

1 December

The weather has been impossible for the last ten days, low cloud and strong wind interspersed with rain storms − practically no flying. Attwood, a new arrival, carried out a trial flight on the 'school' bus and had to land at Coudekerque with water pump trouble. My leave is through at last and at this time of the year it doesn't look as if I shall miss much in the way of operations. I left by the 10.45 am destroyer, *Falcon*, which didn't actually leave until 11.15, waiting for a belated 'brass hat'. Very rough in the Channel, so much so that we had to reduce to fifteen knots and even then we seemed to be as much under the water as on top. We were all feeling pretty sorry for ourselves after the first hour or so. Reached Dover at 2.45 pm and, it being impossible to get a taxi, missed the 3.30 to town, catching the 5.45 after a good tea in the Burlington. Fixed up at Morley's Hotel and dined and spent the evening with my uncle and aunt.

Ran into Victor Sieveking and together we visited the Admiralty and arranged about the investiture on 12 December. Having decided on a binge in town for a few days before returning to France on 15 December, I booked accommodation at Morley's for my people and myself and went down to my home in Gloucestershire for a few days. In due course we all migrated to London for six festive days during which we did some eight shows, feasted at the most exciting places and attended the investiture on the 12th, Sieveking and I collecting the necessary swords from Gieves. Amongst those attending were Collishaw (DSO), Norton, Enstone, Sieveking and myself (DSCs). The King looked very tired and spoke in a subdued voice − how sick he must get of shaking hands and saying a few words to each one! It was all over, as far as I was concerned, by 11 am when Sieveking and I walked out and braved the lined-up crowd and press photographers. After linking up with various relatives and disposing of our swords, we mustered a large luncheon party at the Trocadero and then went on to His Majesty's where I had booked umpteen seats for *Chu Chin Chow* − a great show and wonderfully staged. Sieveking came with us. Next day I had to see Brewerton, the Harley Street eye specialist, who was extremely nice and diagnosed nothing worse than eye strain and slight astigmatism. He absolutely refused to take a fee from 'one of our flying boys' as he termed me. Thereafter I lunched at Simpsons with Sieveking and 'Tommy' who has grown a beard and looks a veritable 'Captain Kettle'. Tea with my people at the Carlton and, after dinner, we went to see *General Post* at the Haymarket. Amongst other shows seen were *Dear Brutus* and *Billetted*. Our final evening we wound up with coffee and liqueurs at the Carlton, where the music was delightful.

As a member of the famous 'Naval 8' Sopwith Triplane squadron, Raymond Collishaw shot down 60 EA, becoming Britain's number three ace. However, of the five top British scorers he was the only one not to be awarded the VC. Was his lack of recognition due in part to the often malicious rivalry at senior level between the RFC and the RNAS?

15 December

All good things come to an end and, after a really wonderful leave enjoyed with many relatives and friends, Sieveking and I caught the 9.20 am for Dover and, finding the destroyer had left, we rang up the aerodrome and found there was a DH to be taken over. Lunched in the Mess, meeting Clarke, St John and Le Mesurier who is as full of life as ever and somewhat thrilled at having flown the Dolphin this morning.* Also saw Wright who has been snaffled from 5 Squadron to take on a Flight in 6(N) Squadron, which is forming with McLaren as CO. I secured DH4, A7742, to take across and Sieveking, who was to have come in the back with me, discovered there was a BE to go over to 14(N) Squadron and took that instead, taking off at 3.15 pm. I left twenty minutes later and in ten minutes was off Calais at 10,000. Sieveking was just landing at Coudekerque as I turned in over Petite Synthe. Very cold trip and difficulty in keeping up the temperature on the way down. Landed at 4.5 pm in gathering dusk.

18 December

A clear and frosty day and very cold with a Force 5 north-east wind. I took up N6000 with Carter to test conditions at 10.20 am. Progress very slow against the wind and extraordinarily bumpy near the ground, so raid temporarily delayed. Morel of 12 Squadron crashed badly on a Camel which stalled on a turn about 50ft. It was about half an hour before he could be extricated after much sawing and chopping, but he very luckily escaped with severe bruises and cuts. And last night an FE.8 was flying round very low with lights on, evidently lost. He

---

* Sopwith 5F.1 Dolphin – a single-seater fighter fitted with a 200hp Hispano-Suiza engine, the wings having backward stagger and an open space above the cockpit to give a pilot the best possible view.

had several attempts to get in and eventually crashed badly, hitting a tree and then the ground at 60mph. We heard the smash from here.

Eight of us, myself leading on N6000, left at 1.40 pm for Engel aerodrome and ammunition dump. Sproatt led the three fighters. Formation good considering the large raw element and we crossed the Lines north of Dixmude at 13,500ft. AA heavy and, near target, very accurate. All the Bessoneaux had been removed from the aerodrome which appeared to be quite deserted, so we attacked the dump. A good line from north-west to south-east and Jackson put one 50lb and four 16lb right on the sheds, straddling the whole dump. Lupton also got some direct hits. A gradual turn after dropping enabled the formation to keep well together. Two formations of fighters came up at us on the way home and we put in some useful shooting at them at longish range. One formation of four followed us to the Lines some 1,500ft above us, but they didn't seem anxious for a scrap. Sproatt, however, claimed to have shot an EA down in flames and his gunlayer, Naylor, to have accounted for another of the first formation. Enemy aircraft over, as usual, between 5.30 and 7.30 pm and a large number of bombs dropped, causing a big fire somewhere in the neighbourhood of the docks.

19 December

Clear, frosty day and again very cold. I led off seven bombers, together with three fighters led by Sproatt, at 11.40 am for Vlisseghem. Following the coast well out to sea, we turned in over Wenduyne at 14,000. AA as usual extremely heavy and accurate, some bursts being horribly close and I could at once see numerous tears in our wings. We dropped on a good line but our bombs fell just short and, making a steady right-hand turn, I headed for the coast at a moderate speed to enable the formation to close. Unfortunately several at the rear of the formation dashed out to sea at speed, only Lupton, McBain and one other keeping formation. Meanwhile our fighters were behind and I could not leave them in order to overtake the others. However, we all closed up over Ostend. When off Middlekerke I suddenly observed what looked like a DH, some distance behind, going down in a vertical dive and, after a few seconds, there was a violent explosion and the whole aircraft flew to bits and fell in 5 or 6 scattered portions − a very nasty sight. I saw no sign of any attacking aircraft, nor were we experiencing any appreciable AA at the time. Richardson and gunlayer Furby failed to return, so it may have been them, though Sproatt claims to have shot down an EA in that area and my impression was that it looked a bit small for a DH. Others at the back of our formation report having seen a DH some 2,000ft below us firing distress signals, so maybe

Richardson is down in enemy waters. Enemy aircraft over again between 5.30 and 7.30 pm.

20 December
Bitterly cold all day and awoke to find everything frozen, including paraffin in the stove! Thick fog rendered flying impossible. The CO and Sproatt went to Calais to examine an aeroplane wheel picked up in the sea off Gravelines. It was a DH wheel but not off one of our aircraft. Five Blimps* from Polegate missing — lost in the fog but reported to be in our locality, so we sent up rockets and had the searchlight working at 8pm.

22 December
After two days of thick fog it has cleared somewhat and I took Stringer up in N5993 for a test at 10.30 am. Climbed through 2,000ft of thick cloud, no gaps, up to 5,000. Did not see the ground for thirty minutes and came through again over Audrycke dump, which seems to have suffered badly from fire, two long rows of sheds being charred and blackened skeletons. After lunch I took up our new army DH4, A7744, for test. 10,000ft in fourteen minutes — nothing to shout about! Extremely cold and difficult to maintain temperature on the way down. Enemy aircraft over just after 5 pm and kept up their 'entertainment' until 10 pm. Freezing hard.

23 December
Very cold again, with a north-east wind. Greeve of 12 Squadron killed on a Camel this morning, clouds at 50ft through which he came diving straight into the ground. He lived just long enough for them to get him to the Alexandra hospital where his sister is a VAD, but never recovered consciousness. Wright of 10 Squadron also killed on a Camel. Looks as if his elevator must have jammed as he made a circuit and a half, stalling all the time with his tail right down, the machine literally hanging in the air. He then apparently shut off in the hope that the nose would drop, but the machine simply tail-slid and spun from 800ft. The Camels are certainly causing a lot of casualties. They need very careful handling low down, especially on a left-hand turn when the engine torque is liable to put them into a spin if the air speed is allowed to fall.

24 December
Thick mist and drizzle all day and milder. Two ailerons and other bits

* Non-rigid airships of the RNAS

of wreckage of DH, N6008, picked up by a monitor 10-15 miles out to sea off Middlekerke, were brought over from the docks. A flying helmet with goggles attached was found on part of the wreckage which rather points to the likelihood of Richardson or his gunlayer being alive after the machine hit the water. Little hope for either of them I fear. Much serenading and carol singing until midnight.

25 December, Christmas Day
Very cold with strong north wind. Celebration of Holy Communion at 11 am. A footer match at 11.45 am, officers versus petty officers, which the latter won easily 3-0 after a comic game. Three or four of our side had never played soccer before and kept handling the ball! We were all very short of wind and done up at the end. Blizzards and snowstorms all the evening. Our Xmas dinner at 7 pm and followed a very hilarious evening. We all plodded through the snow to 12 Squadron at 10.30 pm and found them decidedly merry. We dragged them all back to 5 Squadron and sent them home still merrier after sampling our punch bowl. We blacked Cleggy's face and he and I went round to B Flight Mess to see how the men were faring and taste their beer which was running freely. We sent them round four bottles of whisky so I think they did pretty well as I had sent them a supply of smokes in the afternoon. We carried on till midnight by which time Cleggy and Carter had to be assisted to bed, the former, however, escaped and found his way to C Flight Mess where he started making speeches at 12.30 or so. Two good photos (groups) were taken in the Officers' Mess at around 11pm, by which time we were all looking pretty well oiled!

28 December
Fine overhead early but thick cloud banks coming up from the north-east. I tested N5992 at 10.30 with Stringer in behind. Very bumpy and heavy, ominous clouds at 4,000. The country under a thick mantle of snow. I drove over to Coudekerque in the CO's car at 5.30 pm and dined with Sieveking and others. A very cold slippery drive, the roads like glass.

29 December
A bright frosty morning and we had all aircraft out and engines running for a raid on Ghistelles which is now in use again. A signal came through, however, from 2(N) Squadron, that thick clouds were over Ostend and coming up from the north-east so I went up on A7744 with Mason to test the conditions. Thick clouds all over Belgium at 3,000ft so I returned and washed out the raid. The sky was completely overcast

and threatening snow by 1.30pm. Sproatt and Cleghorn go on Canadian leave (two months) tomorrow.

31 December

Bright early but clouds soon completely overcast the sky. 'Make and mend' for the starboard watch after lunch. Lupton, Pat and I walked round the château and canal bridge before dinner and felt better for some exercise — roads most frightfully slippery. New Year's Eve and the deuce of a full-out one, started by numerous 'knock-downs' for drinks during dinner and continued throughout the evening, conditions becoming more and more lively. At 9.30 pm we went over and raised hell at 12 Squadron and most of them came back and were thoroughly well doped in our Mess. At midnight we turned out and rang the inside out of the Ship's bell, and that turned all the ratings out who, forming a circle, danced round us singing *Auld Lang Syne* at the top of their voices. Luppy and I then managed to get hold of the CO and drag him into the centre. We then sent out about a dozen of champagne to the men and John Gamon, Mason and I roused Petty Officers Clark and Langford, B Flight's chief fitter and rigger, and we all drank to B Flight. On returning we found a crowd milling round the Wardroom and were soon being carried round shoulder high. Williams then started up the HQ car which was standing outside the Mess and drove round to 12 Squadron, with the brakes fairly hard on it was afterwards discovered, taking with him Hughes, Goldie and one or two more. Hughes returned in a wheelbarrow and was wheeled by Potts into the Wardroom. They had found 12 all gone to bed. After this it was discovered that several members of the Mess had disappeared and a rush was made for their cabins and those who had been foolish enough to lock their doors had them broken down and were hauled out. Further hot punch was dispensed and it was 2.30 am before we finally cleared the Mess and thought about bed. I turned in about 3.30. John Gamon stood by his Flight Commander like a brick but did not have to help him to bed! Perhaps the most full-out night I'm ever likely to remember.

9

Spoiling Attacks

1 January, 1918

Oh, what a head! Tilling scared me stiff with the news that it was a nice clear morning when he called me, but thank Heaven it clouded over and I didn't turn out till 12.30. Lupton, Pat and I again walked round the château walk after lunch and felt much revived. I turned in early.

3 January

Bright early and we started getting aircraft out until a heavy snowstorm drove them under cover again. It cleared a bit at midday and I led off at 1.15 pm on N6004 for Ghistelles just as another snowstorm came up and was in the thick of it at 500ft. However, heading hard for the blue I outpaced it and so did five others who followed, the remainder not leaving the ground until considerably later. Getting height around Cassel, the wind proved so strong that at 90 knots we were hardly making any progress at 12,000ft and as another storm was coming up I had to signal the washout and then, with a storm raging over Dunkirk, wait for it to pass before attempting a landing. The fighters had returned within half an hour of leaving the ground, with the exception of Dixon who turned up just on dusk having gone off on one of his solo stunts again, much to everyone's annoyance.

4 January

A sunny morning and sharp frost. Eight bombers and three fighters, myself leading on N6000, took off at 10.10 am for Ghistelles. Very good formation with the exceptions of Williams and Attwood who never got up to the rest of the formation despite my holding up for them, Attwood eventually turning back. Strong north wind up top and we crossed the Lines at 14,500 a little south of Nieuport, arriving over the target at 11.15 at 15,000. AA very heavy and at times accurate. Naylor, my new gunlayer, obtained one direct hit and several more close as we led a tight formation on a good line across the target, which, being well straddled, must have suffered considerable damage. Making a very gradual turn for home, the formation kept well together and never lost their places, but the fighters were too far behind and only on our level instead of 500ft above. However, no EA materialized. My throttle jammed a third open on our way back so that I didn't close down below 1200 revs and had considerable difficulty in getting down eventually, having to switch off all mags and land at Coudekerque. A landing across the aerodrome into a north wind at Petite Synthe would have been hazardous. I lunched in 14 Squadron's Mess — nearly everybody away on a joy ride to Armentières. After getting the throttle fixed I landed at Petite Synthe at 3 pm.

A DH4 is reported to have dropped bombs on St Pol village this morning, obliterating a house. Apparently Mason's gunlayer, a new man over the Lines for the first time, had such wind up when we were being heavily shelled that he was quite incapable of rational action and brought all his bombs back, signalling to Mason as he was about to land or go out to sea. He then pulled off several miles before they had crossed the coast, evidently making no allowance for the strong north wind. He was in a very rattled state when they landed and is obviously quite useless as a gunlayer. There is sure to be an almighty strafe and an inquiry. That is the sort of man we get sent out now as a trained gunlayer!

6 January
A doubtful morning but fairly clear overhead. I took up N5974 at 11.45 am to test conditions. Visibility the far side of the Lines possible though not good, and a stiff west wind to battle home against. Thick clouds, coming up from the west, were overhead within ten minutes of my landing so the raid was washed out. Conditions quite impossible by 2 pm. A delightful surprise for me this evening when my chief rigger and fitter, Petty Officers Langford and Clark, presented me with a beautiful silver cigarette case, suitably engraved from all the ratings of B Flight. It is touching to think that these men, many of whom are earning only three or four shillings a day, should subscribe three or four guineas to present me with such a handsome token of their goodwill. It is something that I shall value and be proud of all my life, and a splendid souvenir of the war and of B Flight in particular. I can't think what I have done to warrant such generosity, having been their CO for only two months. They are a splendid lot of fellows and it is a great joy to have such men under one.

7 January
Overcast all day. B and C Flights busy getting a new cover on the middle Bessoneau. A new pilot for A Flight arrived from 12 Squadron. Lupton and I walked up beyond the bridge and back in the afternoon, meeting a nice fellow, Lieutenant Moore from the chink's camp in the

château grounds, who made us come in and have tea in their Mess. Captain Garson, their CO, is a delightful man and we sat talking until 6 pm. Hope we will see more of them.

10 January

A strong penetrating north-east wind for the last three days. St John arrived from Dover to supervise the building of quarters for 6 Naval Squadron. Wing Commander's inspection this morning after which he stopped for lunch. A jolly evening. Our car had no headlights so we went up to 7 Squadron to rout out one of theirs, but found them busy round the roulette board and got involved.

11 January

Raining heavily in the morning but had stopped by 10 am when I took up N6000, with Petty Officer Clark in the back, to test after carburettor overhaul. Clouds of the dark misty variety from 600ft upwards. Climbed through to 5,000 with very occasional glimpses of the ground — none at all after 2,500. Layer after layer apparently going up indefinitely. Landed in a drizzle. It cleared a bit after lunch and one or two test flights were carried out. Wing Captain Lambe visited us at about 3 pm but did not stop long.

13 January

Sunday. A day of disasters. Nine of us attempted to take off at 10 am for Engel dump. There was a stiff north-west wind but, our aircraft being lined up facing due west, i.e. along the length of the aerodrome, I led off 45 degrees out of the wind and pulled it off all right, though the wind, drifting one to port, made it none too easy and the bumps were very bad near the ground. Omerod, seeing what a big drift there was, waved to Willis to taxi into the corner and take off more into wind, but Willis apparently misunderstood the signal and attempted to take off still more cross-wind. The wind slewed him round still further and, with very little run, he tried to hoik over the railway trucks in the timber yard, stalled, his port wing hit a truck and the machine instantly burst into flames. Poor Willis was very badly burned before they could get him out. I, of course, knew nothing of all this and wondered at the cause of the delay. After a few minutes, however, the remainder took off and formed up on me, Attwood and one of the fighters dropping out before we crossed the Lines at 13,000. We therefore crossed only six strong and soon reached the target, Naylor planting three of our bombs plumb in the middle of the dump. Immediately after dropping, seven menacing EA passed just below us and we got in some distant shots at them. I was a bit more nervous about them as our formation was distinctly straggly, our fighters having allowed themselves to be drifted much too far south in the face of a strong north-west wind and we had a long enough journey to the Lines more or less in the teeth of the wind. But I need not have worried as they were a cold-footed crowd and took no chances of coming near us. Indeed we had cause to be grateful to them as AA was consequently light, whereas had they not been hovering around, we should have had Hell, the day being clear and ourselves slow-moving targets. Mason and I got a few bursts near us but it was never enough to worry us.

I landed at 1 pm, knowing nothing till then of Willis's crash. The wreckage was still burning and the bombs had been going off at intervals, two or three of our men being wounded while endeavouring to save the French rolling stock. All the French 'Tommies' ran like rabbits the moment they knew there were bombs on board. The first 50lb bomb went off a minute or two after they got Willis and Foster clear. The latter sustained a broken leg and Willis pulled himself out of the burning wreckage but, being blinded, fell back into the flames. They rushed him down to the Queen Alexandra (hospital) very badly burned about the face and arms and it is feared he may never recover his sight, even if he gets over the shock – he never lost consciousness. I'm frightfully sorry about him, he was such a good fellow. It should never have happened, seeing the way the wind had skidded me sideways. He should have switched off the moment he found himself slewing towards the timber yard. The signal also should have been given in such a way as to be unmistakable. Mason, Gamon and I strolled over towards the still-burning mass after lunch when the final 16lb bomb went off. A gunlayer who, against orders, was trying to salvage a burnt Lewis gun, had a leg and arm blown off and died a few hours later in hospital. Just after this the fire alarm sounded as Drummond's cabin was found to be on fire – fortunately quickly got under control and not much damage. A most unlucky 13th – and a Sunday too.

14 January

A heavy fall of snow in the night. It was fairly clear after lunch when McBain and I took up new gunlayers to test their capabilities. I took Middleton to and along the Lines, landing in semi-mist at 3.45 pm. McLaren arrived together with a few Flight Sub-Lieutenants and ground personnel for 6(N) Squadron.

15 January

Deluges of rain most of the day. Funeral of Jeffries, the gunlayer, at 2.30

pm. John Gamon and I busy auditing the Mess accounts. Poor Willis passed away at 5.10 pm. We all feel his loss very much. He was a favourite with everybody. The whole place more or less under water this evening. A violent hurricane sprang up very suddenly about 11 pm and raged furiously all night. Little chance of sleep and at 2.45 am I got up and fought my way round to our Bessoneaux to see they were secured all right. Our middle one would have gone for a certainty had we not put on the new top over the old one the other day. One of 6(N) Squadron's new Bessoneaux carried away completely, but luckily the two DH4s inside were undamaged due to prompt action.

16 January
We are more or less marooned in floods. 6 Squadron's Bessoneaux have eighteen inches of water in them, the aerodrome is half under water and the tennis court quite a deep lake with ducks swimming about on it. It rained most of the day. We all attended Willis's funeral at 2.30 pm. It is very sad to think he has gone from us. We could spare him least of all the new pilots.

19 January
Overcast and threatening all day. I walked into Dunkirk after lunch, did some shopping and met John Gamon and Drummond for tea at Goberts. Le Mesurier and Clarke arrived from Dover on the new 200hp DHs. Clarke is permanently for 6(N) Squadron. Le M dined at Wing HQ; nice to see him again. Although completely overcast, EA paid us a visit between 6 and 7 pm. AA very heavy and a number of bombs fell around. From the noise of their engines they can't have been above 2-3,000ft.

20 January
Deluged all day. Le Mesurier returned to Dover by the midday destroyer. A case of scarlet fever amongst 6(N)'s ratings has caused all their officers to leave our Mess forthwith. A pretty rowdy evening, dinner consisting of a series of 'knock-downs'. Goldie (Goldsmith) got it for the first time on record and it cost him 40-odd ports. I caught it three times and St John any number, consequently drinks flowed somewhat liberally!

21 January
Another dud day, wind and rain up to teatime when it cleared to a priceless moonlight evening with a stiff south wind, consequently two very lively hours from 11.15 to 1.15 am. Enemy aircraft paid incessant visits and were flying very low, consequently the AA barrage was

extremely noisy, being so close overhead. A large number of bombs dropped and the whole area illuminated by parachute flares. With the exception of Lupton, Omerod, Dickson and myself, the whole Mess apparently congregated in two feet of water in the dugout – we preferring bed. Fortunately we were well blacked out and (apparently) their bombers didn't spot us, there being no water or prominent landmark to show us up at night. One of our Hun visitors of the 19th was brought down by AA near Furnes.

22 January
Rain early and overcast all day. At 2.30 pm we essayed to do a formation flight primarily with the object of training a number of new gunlayers and also to afford practice in formation – keeping to the new pilots. The aerodrome was very heavy with mud and pools of water. I managed to take old N5993 off dead across the 'drome with plenty to spare. Attwood who followed appeared to steer a course through every patch of water he could find and then tried to stagger off more or less side to wind with a badly splintered propeller, giving another hair-raising exhibition over the wood yard and crashing undercarriage and lower planes in a small field. I saw it all happen from the air. Omerod quite rightly washed the stunt out for the others, so after circling and diving low over the crash to see that there was no serious damage, I made off to the Lines and had an interesting time watching considerable activity along the Nieuport-Dixmude front, thereby giving a new gunlayer, Leitch, plenty of opportunity for doing some spotting. It was extremely clear and one could see the whole of Belgium right up to the Dutch frontier. An old twin-engined Caudron and a Belgian 1½ Strutter were being well plastered over Westende and Dixmude respectively and we ran into a formation of Camels over the floods. Landed at 3.45 pm and, whilst taxying, my wheels sank to the axles and I had to be hauled out with full-bore engine.

23 January
Overcast most of the day. I took up a new gunlayer, Watson, for a test flight on N6000 at 11.30 am. Gamon and Mason also came up, and Seidle on the school bus. I went to the Lines and got several long bursts off at a bridge over the Yser at Nacelle and apparently started a fire as a dense column of smoke arose from the bank of the river and continued for four or five minutes. Received some AA but mostly pretty wide, although we were at 3,000ft only. After lunch we tried another formation flight, taking up new gunlayers. I led on N5992 with gunlayer Hooper in the back. Carter, Gamon and Lupton followed but Williams

didn't get off and Dickson, who got stuck in the mud, didn't pick us up until we broke formation. Carter flew too close and kept overshooting. Afterwards I took Hooper down to the Lines and gave him a good look into Hunland. Conditions were not good for formation practice as clouds were at 2,000 and a second layer at 4,000. On returning, clouds were thick from 2,000 down to 150ft and it was extremely bumpy at that height. Landed at 4 pm and not sorry to get on the ground.

24 January

Overcast and heavy rain early but cleared by 11 am, when McBain, Carter, Seidle and I went up for formation practice and to train new gunlayers. McBain and Carter kept very good formation on me but Seidle rather lagged behind. Later I continued to the Lines, landing at 12.45 pm. I had gunlayer Bonser with me. I tested A7663, one of Lupton's A Flight DHs, at 3.15 with another new gunlayer, Cook, in the back. Again to the Lines and back, giving him a good view of enemy territory. Landed at 4 pm just as the CO, Goble, returned from leave, so my responsibilities are over, temporarily at any rate. He brought with him an Australian visitor, Colonel Dugdale.

25 January

Cloud early. I went up at 9.40 on N5974 to take Colonel Dugdale for a joy ride and to test weather conditions. He had never flown before so I did a fairly straightforward flight. Thin clouds at 2,000ft all over Belgium with few gaps, but this all cleared off as the sun gained strength and at 12.20 pm I led a formation of nine for Varssenaere, Gamon and Dickson acting as fighters. Formation very good but Williams dropped out at 12,000 and Seidle, who was much slower and considerably behind, despite my throttling down and holding up the rest of the formation to enable him to catch up, turned back just before we crossed the Lines at 15,000, reaching our target at 15,500 at 1.30 pm. AA was very heavy and alarmingly accurate over the target and all the way back to the lines. Eleven hits on our machine and Mason and McBain on my immediate right and left were also badly strafed. Mac had his flying coat ripped by a chunk of HE. About as bad a shelling as I have experienced, we must have heard at least 50 crashes and the machine fairly quivered at times. Four Hun scouts passed some 2,000ft below us but had no chance to pick us up as we were in much too good formation for them. Good results were obtained despite the shelling. We landed at 2.18 pm and were not sorry to be back in one piece. The German AA really is extremely good nowadays provided they are able to see us clearly.

Before leaving this morning an official photo was taken of the CO and Colonel Dugdale, flanked by myself, Mason and a visiting army officer, in front of my DH4, N5974, with Petty Officer Clark in the cockpit doing a final check. Large numbers of enemy aircraft passed overhead and were welcomed with a violent barrage, but apparently they were on their way to Blighty. Just after turning in at 10.30 pm the Leugenboom gun opened up, plonking over her 15in shells at regular seven-minute intervals and, as an aircraft was circling overhead evidently spotting for her, it looked as if she was trying to get us. We prepared for a warm time but she packed up at midnight and there were no further disturbances to mar our slumbers. We learn that a Gotha was forced down and captured, the pilot being shot in the face.

27 January
Ten of us left at 12.15 pm for Aertrycke, I myself being given a special target, Engel dump. One bomber and one fighter dropped out when we were getting height over Calais and Williams crossed the Lines some 2,000ft below the rest of the formation. What we took to be thick clouds, but eventually proved to be fog, covered the whole country below us and precluded all possibility of picking up our targets, so we dropped our bombs by compass and watch rather than bring them all back. Williams lost himself completely and landed in the fog on the beach, 200 yards our side of Nieuport Piers, crashing badly but fortunately without injury to himself or his gunlayer. At 3 pm I took up N5993 with gunlayer Jones to try and see Williams' crash, but we went into thick fog just beyond La Panne at 150ft so turned for home, only to discover that the fog had come up from all directions and completely cut me off from Dunkirk. I tried flying low but could only dimly catch sight of the ground from under 100ft and at times was only 20ft above the sand dunes. I climbed through into sunlight again at 200ft to discover the iron foundry chimneys sticking up through the fog barely 50 yards away to port. That settled me to get down at once in a small clear space I had spotted near the Red hospital, which was quickly disappearing as the fog encroached. Fortunately, the dim outline of a Bessoneau caught my eye and, from 100ft, I landed safely at Bray Dunes two or three minutes before that too was completely blotted out. The fog was so dense that one could only see for a distance of 30 yards on the ground and I was never more thankful to be down. The French housed N5993 and I had tea in their Mess — a jolly nice lot of fellows they are. Jones was looked after by their men and a car rolled up in due course and got us back to 5 Squadron by 7 pm. Ransford on the school bus got caught in the fog and, after

circling for several minutes at 50ft, crashed badly just off the aerodrome, fortunately without injury. A somewhat disastrous day and – as usual – a Sunday!

28 January

I went over to Bray Dunes in the CO's car at 9.15 am, taking with me Leading Mechanic Mason. Collected N5993 at 10.50 am, landing just in time to transfer to 'B1' (N6000) and lead off the formation for Aertrycke aerodrome at 11.28 am with gunlayer Naylor in the back. Two bombers and one fighter dropped out before we reached Calais. Crossed the Lines in good formation at 15,500 and, passing over Coucklaere and Engel, dropped on a good line over the target, Naylor getting a direct hit on a Bessoneau with several more in close proximity to the others. On our return three EA made half-hearted attempts to attack but on our swinging round to do battle they spun away. We got off a whole tray at one at somewhat long range without apparent effect, though we saw our tracers hitting. Several side-loops on our way back and lost our Very pistol and cartridges on one when the old DH stuck on her back. Le Mesurier landed from Dover, having chased imaginary EA over to Nieuport and run more or less out of petrol. Anything for an excuse to get over here! He left again at 3 pm. Major-General Salmond visited us at 3.30 pm with Wing Captain Lambe, and flew off at 4 pm in an Armstrong Whitworth contraption that came to fetch him.*

29 January

A glorious sunny day. I led off a formation for a new objective at 11.55 am. Ransford and Ormerod had trouble with their engines and never got away, so we left as a formation of six bombers and only one fighter, John Gamon. The formation picked up well and we headed up the coast keeping well out to sea. Crossed the coast close to the Dutch frontier at 15,000 and I soon spotted the target, Coolkerke aerodrome, from about Westcappelle. At Dudzele I turned left and followed a course parallel to the Zeebrugge-Bruges canal, getting a good line over the target from north to south. Several of our bombs fell among, and very close up to, the hangars both at the northern and southern ends of the aerodrome. One fire was started by another aircraft among huts just off the aerodrome. AA plentiful and accurate. Very good view of Bruges as we skirted the edge of it. AA again very heavy from Knocke and Blankenberghe until we got well out to sea. Three EA hung around the tail of our formation which was too well closed up for them to venture

---

* This was an A-W.FK8 used for ground attack and reconnaissance by the RFC.

close. Naylor got a tray off at the nearest and our tracers appeared to be hitting, but without visible effect. Just before we took off this morning a German photographic bus was overhead at 19-20,000ft but our AA was nowhere near him.

30 January

A perfect day but very hazy early – and, had I known it, very nearly proving to be my last! Seven bombers and three fighters left at 11.50 am for Oostcamp aerodrome, some five miles south of Bruges. I was first on the right, Lupton leading. Getting height over Calais, an enemy photographic bus was high overhead being vigorously shelled, but AA was nearer to us than to him. We crossed the Lines in good formation at 16,000 and were able to see our objective in the distance from Engel. We got a very good line over the target and obtained a direct hit on a large hangar in the southern corner which went up in flames and several other bombs burst among sheds in the north corner. Immediately after dropping we were heavily engaged by some fifteen to twenty EA which seemed to appear suddenly from nowhere, diving down out of the sun and choosing their attack when our formation was split up after dropping and had not had time to reform. I found three of them on my tail and a fourth came head-on. I had to zoom to avoid him and never had time to use my front guns, but he did and then shot below my port wing and joined the other three on my tail, my engine at the same time cutting out on three cylinders and my revs dropping away to 1,300. I also saw my water temperature gauge shoot up to boiling, the pointer then dropping back to zero, and I realized that my radiator had been hit and all, or most, of the water in it had gone. What chance had I of getting back with a badly-missing engine vibrating like Hell and little or no water to cool it off?

The Dutch frontier looked near and for a moment I was tempted, but the thought of internment for the rest of the war decided me to try for home or die in the attempt. Meanwhile Naylor was dealing with the four on our tail and, getting one in flames, the other three hung back and fired from a distance, their tracers going wide. How I blessed little Lupton who had seen my predicament and held the formation tight closed and as slow as possible and, although already some distance away to my north, enabled me to dive down and get just ahead of the formation, though already much lower. I expected every moment to be shot up from under the tail as, with nose well down, Naylor could not possibly cover that position. Fortunately for me some of those EA seemed to be as poor pilots as they were cold-footed and now at last, ahead of the formation, I could at least be seen, though steadily losing height. The engine was missing, banging and vibrating to such an extent that I expected it to cut out altogether at any moment and to have to spin down into enemy territory, but she gamely held on with her 12-1300 revs. Over Ghistelles, being then some 4,000ft below and just ahead of the formation, I spotted three more EA about 800ft below me. To my relief and amazement they made no attempt to attack, and I can only imagine that, seeing the formation sitting high above, they took me for a decoy and weren't having any. Never was I more relieved to cross the floods and, after the tension of never expecting to make the Lines, I regarded 'Archie' at my low height in quite friendly spirit − an almost welcome companion after those enemy fighters. I actually managed to make and land on the aerodrome with my radiator empty and my engine so hot that our fitters could not get near it − why it never seized is a miracle. A bullet had severed the induction port feeding the front three starboard cylinders and another had made a mess of the radiator. It speaks volumes for the old Rolls Eagle VII engine.

John Gamon got an explosive bullet in his cockpit which had no more serious result than putting the smoke up him. Carter landed at 9(N) Squadron with his tanks pierced, a landing wire shot away and his coat ripped through and arm bruised by a passing bullet. One of his back Lewis guns was shot off its mounting but his gunlayer, Watson, got rid of it and carried on with the remaining one − a very creditable performance for a new man. Williams has not yet returned and no news at all of him, but I thought I saw him this side of the Lines on the return journey. I fully expected that we would lose two or three of our formation and hardly expected myself to see Dunkirk again. Lupton's good leading, enabling the formation to close right up, was our salvation and but for that I doubt if I should ever have got back. We also owe our return to the poor piloting and lack of thrust on the part of those EA who so greatly outnumbered us when miles over their own territory, having also the great tactical advantage of surprise, diving down all unseen out of the sun. They should have accounted for at least half of us and certainly should never have let me escape.

31 January

Another priceless morning with sharp frost. I led off a formation of six bombers and two fighters for Engel aerodrome and dump at 10.30 am. We crossed the Lines in perfect formation at 16,000 and dropped at that height at 1 pm. Got a direct hit on a small hangar on the western side of the aerodrome and a 50lb on the main railway line at the north of the dump. AA light and inaccurate on account of the thick haze. Four EA seen but too low to attack us. The very thick haze made landing difficult, it being only just possible to spot the aerodrome at 500ft from half a mile away. A thick fog came up at 2 pm and blotted out everything. Still no news of Williams and his gunlayer, Leitch, so I fear he must be down on the wrong side of the Lines, though I'm fairly confident I saw him just our side of the Lines on our return yesterday, so his loss is a mystery. Toby Watkins, a very senior Flight Lieutenant, who has been instructing for years at Eastchurch, joined 5 Squadron today, rather to the dismay of many of our pilots who have done six or eight months active service and, naturally, feel they are being passed over (for promotion) by someone who is out from England for the first time. Nevertheless, he is a very good fellow and a fine pilot.

2 February
After a day of fog, the sun shines again with only high cirrus clouds. I led a formation of six bombers and two fighters for Varssenaere at 10.30 am. Crossing the Lines at 16,000ft, we again obtained very good results, Naylor setting one hangar on fire and getting the rest of his bombs amongst a group of hangars on the east side of the aerodrome along the edge of the Château wood. Many other explosions observed on the aerodrome, some close to hangars. AA exceedingly heavy and very accurate, nearly every aircraft being hit, while Stringer, John Gamon's observer, got a severe bruise on the shoulder from a spent chunk of HE which cut through his flying coat. Three EA seen below, a large one escorted by two fighters. After lunch I took N6000 up, with gunlayer Burne, to test its performance against a BHP-engined DH piloted by Clarke of 6(N) Squadron. Clarke just beat me for climb up to 15,000ft, speed up top the same, my engine, however, was not going its best. Cooper of HQ came to dinner, bringing with him a French Commandant who was a great sport. Much ragging after dinner.

3 February
Bright early but considerably overcast by 10 am when I took up N6004 to test conditions with the CO, Goble, in the back. Clear of clouds over the Lines, so I led off a formation of seven bombers and two fighters at 11.30 am for Houttave. Lupton dropped out early with pressure trouble. Turned out to sea off La Panne and passed Nieuport piers at 13,000. Crossed the coast at Wenduyne at 15,000. Just before we crossed the coast a DH from another unit was being heavily shelled by Blankenberghe at about 18,000ft, consequently they did not concentrate on us until we were well over the coast and nearly on to our target. Our bombs dropped in a line just in front of the hangars but no direct hit. Stringer claimed a direct hit on the large hangar. AA very heavy and

accurate and, as has happened before on Houttave raids, one pilot, in this instance Ransford, shot underneath me and took several others with him who apparently mistook him for the leader, and led them about fifteen miles out to sea. Mason stuck with me well. The others received a strafing on landing. Carter was attacked by an Albatros scout at about 200 yards range and his gunlayer, Watson, drove him down in a spin from which they did not see him pull out.

4 February

Clouds overhead but clear towards the Lines, so Lupton led seven bombers and two fighters at 9.30 am for Zuidwege ammunition dump. At 15,000 over the Red hospital we were still below the clouds and, two machines having dropped out, Lupton fired the washout signal. Actually we could have got there, or our alternative Engel, but we should have got Hell from AA, being silhouetted against the clouds. Poor Winter folded up on a Camel today while diving on a Hun.

5 February

A doubtful day. Lupton tested conditions early and decided to await developments. I tested them at midday with Lupton in the back and we decided to wash out finally as thick clouds enveloped the whole country over the Lines at 9,000ft and it was appallingly bumpy below them. Several went up after lunch hot air balloon-strafing. Barker landed from Coudekerque in his Handley Page, *Evening Star* at 3 pm. I went up with him taking over control at 2,000ft. It was much like flying a traction engine and on a decent bank you feel she is never coming out, she answers the controls so slowly, otherwise quite easy to fly. I lost my hat overboard, the HP's windscreen not being so effective as Barker made out.

7 February

Rain and wind for two days so I lay in till midday, having felt rotten for the last few days. The Doc says he will fix up a short leave for me – I should be due anyway in another month. Mason and I walked along the canal after tea and met Jones and two others paddling in a punt made out of an old Short float.

14 February

The weather has been impossible for a whole week, rain and wind the whole time. Omerod and I dined one night at Wing HQ with the Wing Commander, Garrett, Fowler and the Doc, having an excellent dinner and a pleasant evening. My leave having come through, I left 5 Squadron at 10.45 am and after fond farewells I saw the Wing Commander just before leaving, who gave me the cheering news that he had recommended me for special confirmation in rank on account of my length of service and that Wing Captain Lambe had approved it — so it only remains for 'Their Lords Commissioners' to sanction. I crossed on the *Leven* together with Garrett and Maund. Fairly rough. Reached Dover 2.15 and, after a hasty lunch at the Burlington, caught the 3.30 to town.

Some 'Pups' provided entertainment at Faversham, and from there up to Chatham, by racing and diving on us and flying alongside us 20ft up, and zooming over trees and houses. They'd have been properly in the soup with a konk and didn't seem expert in throttling a Le Rhone, their engines missing badly all the time.

I spent seven days in town meeting many old friends and seeing a number of shows. I met also my cousin, Vernon Bartlett, whom I had not seen for years and we fixed up various meetings for lunch, dinner etc. Air raid warnings seem to sound most evenings, causing people to scuttle into cellars and the Underground, quite unnecessarily, until the All Clear, when basements poured out people like rats out of holes.

From London I went down to Kent for a few days to look up old friends, and then down to my home near Gloucester for a final twelve days, several of which, together with my parents and sister (whose husband, Graham Weir of the RFC is still a POW in Germany, having been shot down in June, 1915), were spent in great comfort at the Lygon Arms, Broadway, where we met very many old friends and visited scenes of our youth, my father having been then Rector of that charmingly picturesque village, Willersey, with its village greens and duck pond.

6 March
After fond farewells, I left for London, travelling up with a nice RNVR Lieutenant named Dyson-Skinner who used to be with 11 Kite Balloons Section at Coxyde. After sundry shopping, I went out to Gerrards Cross to spend the night with my cousin, Vernon Bartlett, and his wife at their house Richmond Lodge, set amidst lovely surroundings with a trout stream at the bottom of their garden. The next day was spent in town, lunching at the Gobelins with my friends the Leslies and going on to a very amusing play, *Sleeping Partners* — Seymour Hicks and Madge Lessing.

8 March
Unable to get a taxi — something to do with last night's raid.

Consequently missed the 9.20 am to Dover. Phoned the Admiralty and found the destroyer had left at 8.30 am, so spent the day in town, seeing another matinee, *Inside the Lines*, catching the 7.50 pm to Dover and arriving at the Burlington to find a dance in full swing. Turned in at 11.30 pm.

9 March

The hotel porter failed to call me at 7 am, as ordered, but I fortunately woke at 7.10 am and, after a hurried breakfast, caught the old *Racehorse* at 9 am. Good quick passage and landed at Dunkirk at 11.15 to find no car to meet me. Eventually discovered that 5 Squadron had decamped south to the Somme, being attached to 22nd Wing RFC and stationed on a former German aerodrome at Mons-en-Chaussée, near Péronne. I went out to Malo HQ where I saw Fowler, Travers, Garrett and the Doc and heard, to my joy, that my confirmation of rank as Flight Commander 'for special war service' had just been gazetted. After lunch Travers and I drove to Petite Synthe and I proceeded to pack my kit. 6(N) Squadron have just done their first raid on Engel aerodrome in the morning and had pushed off again on a low stunt to bomb a very large four-engined German aircraft stranded in a field near St Pierre Capelle. Le Mesurier (who is now with 11(N) Squadron, in my old cabin) and Clarke dropped to 1,500ft over the target and put in some effective bombing. Le M was later attacked by six EA but out-dived them. Bannatyne was wounded in two places and his observer hit in the leg by an explosive bullet, but they managed to get down on the beach at Coxyde. Travers has command of 11, much to Le Mesurier's disappointment. I slept in Luppy's old cabin and messed at 6(N) Squadron. I am to travel down to 5 Squadron with a flight of Americans by troop train tomorrow – no aircraft to be flown down and I can't get road transport.

10

We Meet and Engage the Red Baron

10 March

The worst journey ever! I left Dunkirk at 10 am with my gunlayer Naylor and a Lieutenant Egbert of the USAS, in charge of his 45 American ratings. We had to change at Calais and found to our disgust that we could not take the civilian (Paris) train, which was leaving in half an hour for Amiens, but had to go on a troop train at 3 pm from Les Fontainettes. Egbert and I chartered two cabs and carted our personal gear along to Les F, leaving all the men in a YMCA hut. The French cabbies did us down atrociously but we were too fed up to haggle with them and there were no military police around. Found the RTO and arranged for the transport of the men's kit from Calais, discovering from him that we could not get beyond Abbeville tonight. We went back into Calais and lunched at the Sauvage, eventually getting all 45 ratings and gear down to Les Fontainettes at 3 pm.

We left there in a 400-yard-long troop train at 4.30 pm and crawled along at a snail's pace to Boulogne in company with two other quite entertaining officers. Arrived Boulogne at 6 pm and there spent nearly an hour in a siding, reaching Etaples at 8.30 pm, where the four of us went to the Officers' Club and were fortunate to get an excellent dinner. We little realized at the time how badly we should need that meal. We reached Abbeville at midnight, where we bundled out in the pitch dark on the rails, the train having pulled up half a mile beyond the station. Eventually we learned from the RTO that we had to proceed to a railway clearing centre at Romscamp, which proved to be 50 miles off-course, halfway to Rouen. We actually skirted Amiens, doubling back and arriving at Romscamp at 5 am stiff and horribly cold. Weary and ill-tempered, we tumbled out and proceeded to unload and cart all our gear about half a mile to the station offices. By this time it was 6 am and getting light. From the RTO we learned our train would not leave for Péronne before 4 pm, so we got the best breakfast we could at a Forces canteen just behind the station, meeting there a nice army officer also bound for Péronne.

There being no accommodation of any sort in which to get a rest in Romscamp, the three of us caught a train to the next station down the line at Abancourt where, above the station buffet, we managed to procure three beds and turned in at 9.15 am. At 2 pm we caught a train back to Romscamp. We were wise to lay in a very good tea at the canteen as the train for Péronne was not leaving until 8 pm. Egbert and I walked up through the village of Romscamp and back, feeling better after three miles of exercise after our ghastly journey. At 7 pm we boarded the train making all possible arrangements for comfort and, managing to get a first class compartment to ourselves, were able to stretch full-length after supping off biscuits and chocolate, tucked up in our trench coats against the cold. I said 'first class' but it was the worst 'first class' I've ever travelled in, old, dilapidated and greasy, our only illumination being from guttering candles placed on the arm rests. We courted sleep without much success. At midnight we pulled up at Chaulnes where distant activity to the east was clearly visible and audible. Turning north there for Péronne, we both at last dropped off and sometime later I awoke to the realisation that we were again halted – it was Péronne at last and 2 am on 12 March.

12 March
I roused Egbert who was snoring like a trooper and we once again proceeded to unload in the dark. The USA ratings were gathered like excited schoolboys round numerous shell craters in the road and the blitzed station. No transport to meet us and, after frantic telephoning, I managed to get through to 5 Squadron who had instructions to meet us at 7 am. I told the telephone orderly to raise the whole station if necessary in order to get transport along at once. In the meantime, leaving a guard over the gear, the three of us walked up to the Officers' Club which exists at one of the less-battered mansions of the place and there procured coffee, bread, butter and jam. In the lounge every seat, easy chair and table was occupied by officers trying to get some sort of rest, many lying full-length on the floor. Little hope there so at 5.30 Egbert and I strolled around the battered remains of the town, having a look at the shell of the cathedral and continuing through half-demolished streets to the station. Transport still 'na pu'* so I walked back and had a look at the old Citadel and several other interesting relics in this much-battered town to which a few civilians are now returning. Our transport rolled up at 7.20 – two lorries and a tender – and we got under way at 7.30, following the banks of the

* First World War slang, derived from *Il n'y en a plus*: There is no more of it. Usually 'napoo'.

Somme to Brie, where we turned east over the bridge along the Amiens–St Quentin road. Brie is smashed almost beyond recognition. We soon passed the ruins of Mons-en-Chaussée and reached 5 Squadron at 8.15 am — 46¼ hours after leaving Dunkirk, a distance of 80 miles as the crow flies! Certainly the longest and most uncomfortable journey I ever want to do.

Grand to see all the old crowd again — four new Flight Sub-Lieutenants, Taylerson, Cartmel, Carroll and Wodehouse, and one observer, Sub-Lieutenant Scott. They seem to be rather a fine crash brigade, Taylerson having crashed three times in four flights and Carroll twice, though nothing serious; while Wodehouse lost himself on his first raid and roamed the country for four days, did the same on his second and has been roaming ever since! I was glad to have a good breakfast, after which I watched eleven of our aircraft take off for Etreux aerodrome (enemy night bombers). I turned in immediately afterwards to try and snatch some rest till 2 pm. I'm fixed up in Omerod's cabin temporarily. I walked round the aerodrome after tea with John Gamon and Mason — a good-sized 'drome but bad surface. Jolly got shot up badly this morning, his gunlayer being hit in the leg, his tanks pierced and controls cut. He landed away. Carter was hit in the neck by a bullet which just grazed his windpipe.

13 March

A good formation sent off again to Etreux at 8.30 am. I got up at 9.30 and, together with Potts and two fitters, left in the tender for Villers Brettoneux at 11 am to collect Seidle's DH which had been left behind when 5 Squadron left that aerodrome where they had been stationed for their first week. An interesting run along the old Grand Prix road to Amiens, Villers Bretonneux being nine miles short of that city. At Brie one crosses the Somme and traverses the old Somme battlefield, the country for ten miles through Estrées and Foucaucourt being pounded to bits and the villages levelled. We reached Villers Bretonneux at 12.00 and soon started up A7857. My old friend George Chester of pre-war days is now with 27 Squadron (RFC) and had just landed from a 4¼ hours photographic reconnaissance. I lunched in their Mess and left at 3.30 pm, following the road back to Mons and, continuing to St Quentin, explored the Lines to the south of that town, landing at 4 pm to find the squadron had pushed off a second raid to Etreux, from which all returned at 6 pm having obtained several direct hits.

14 March

A dull and misty morning clearing somewhat after lunch. Nothing doing, however, the visibility being very poor. Lupton, Watkins and I put in a good walk past 35 Squadron RFC to Mereaucourt and along the valley towards Tertry, returning over the downs.

15 March
A fine clear morning and nine of us left at 9.30 am, led by Watkins, for Bohain aerodrome and dump. We gained height around Péronne, Albert and Amiens and crossed the Lines at 15,000. AA light but fairly accurate. Unfortunately, my guiding 'reins' (our only means of steering a good line) jammed and we didn't get the best possible traverse. Naylor, however, scored one direct hit causing a fire. On our return I diverted down to St Quentin and just north of the town four enemy two-seaters striped black and white crossed some 3-400ft over my tail. Unfortunately our back guns jammed after four rounds and so they were away in the distance before Naylor could let them have a burst at long range, otherwise two of them were sitting targets. Landed at 11.45 am after exploring the Lines down as far as La Fère. Eleven of us left again at 3.15 pm, Lupton leading, for Etreux. Mason dropped out before crossing the Lines. The target was very clearly visible from 16,000ft. It was exceedingly bumpy which didn't improve one's aim, some fairly good shooting, however. I was flying N5961 which was missing badly at times but got me through all right. Landed just before 5 pm. An enemy photographic bus was overhead at a great height after lunch, and just before dinner one of our kite balloons went down in flames. Wodehouse returned this morning after a 'tour' of many days all over France!

16 March
I led off eight bombers and three fighters at 9.45 am for Busigny aerodrome and dump, with instructions to circle the target after dropping to draw the enemy up to be dealt with by twelve SE5As of 84 Squadron RFC, who would be sitting in the sun, waiting to fall on them. We got height round Péronne, Albert and Villers Bretonneux and ten of us crossed the Lines in good formation just south of Le Catelet at 10.45 am and were soon over the target, which showed up clearly. Naylor got eight of our bombs right on the dump, the remaining four falling just off the aerodrome. After dropping I took the formation round in large sweeping circles between Bohain and Le Cateau for twenty minutes, waiting for the SE5As to put in an appearance, but they let us down badly — though we certainly drew the enemy up for them had they been there. By this time our rear machines were getting straggled and being engaged by numbers of EA, so I headed for the Lines,

throttling down and holding up to 50 knots to enable all aircraft to close up. We got off 100 rounds at two EA who came in close and drove them off. The front of the formation kept well together, but the rear machines straggled despite our low speed and were heavily engaged. Dickson and Gamon were badly shot up, the former having petrol tanks pierced, spars shot through and many holes through his fuselage; and John (Gamon) was equally badly strafed. Cartmel with Wilcox and Omerod with 'Pat' failed to return. One of them was seen going down with about ten EA on his tail. As we were at the time some ten miles over the Lines with a strong west wind to battle against, I deemed it best to keep the remainder of the formation together and head slowly for home, giving stragglers every chance to pick up with us.

The Wing Commander (22nd Wing, RFC) Colonel F. V. Holt, and the CO of 84 Squadron, Major Sholto Douglas [later Lord Douglas of Kirtleside] came over to lunch to talk things over. They seemed well satisfied with our part of the business. The whole trouble was the SE5As failed to synchronize, arriving much too late when the battle was in fact over. News came through in the evening that Cartmel had landed at Amiens slightly wounded. No news of Omerod. One of our AA gunners says he saw a DH4 go down out of control the wrong side of the Lines. It looks bad. 62 Squadron (RFC) sent out a formation of eight the other day and none returned. They lost fifteen in three days but accounted for many more. 84 Squadron have claimed 90 EA in six weeks.

17 March
Nine of us left again for Busigny at 10.23 am, led by Watkins, with the same instructions, ourselves acting as bait to draw the enemy up for the SE5As to deal with. We crossed the Lines at 15,000 over Belle Église and, approaching Bohain, observed a rare old mix-up already in progress between some fifteen SE5As and about twenty Huns. The SEs were having it pretty much their own way, their opponents spinning down in all directions with SEs on their tails. It was a glorious sight; several Huns went down in flames and in all the Squadron accounted for eight certainties without loss to themselves. We got four direct hits on the dump and, thanks to the SE5As, were unmolested. AA on the way light but accurate.

> Watkins, in his diary, wrote, "Had to take the formation through the clouds when getting our height and then steer by compass. Luckily the clouds cleared over the Lines and found I was on my course but with only four of the nine machines which started, the others having lost themselves

in the clouds or returned with engine trouble. Saw large formation of Huns waiting for us over the target but I pretended not to see them and carried on — very brave! Fact was, I could see the SE5s up above between the Huns and the sun. The Huns manoeuvred to get under our tails and in a few seconds the SEs were on to them. Then ensued the biggest scrap I've ever seen. The sky seemed full of machines, looping, cartwheeling, spinning, diving in flames, and going down without their wings. Saw one Hun go down in a vertical dive for 15,000ft and crash in the middle of a village. The net result was 8 Huns bagged, without a single British loss. Some of our DH4s badly shot up, but no one wounded and all returned."

At 3.30 pm I took up Egbert for a test flight in N5992. We toured round Ham, St Quentin, Bapaume, Albert and Péronne and flew very low over Bapaume and the two enormous mine craters at Pozières. Descending to 1,000ft over Albert, we clearly saw the gilded statue of the Virgin so miraculously suspended from the top of the tower, leaning below the horizontal over the street. The French believe that when it falls the war will end.

> In fact the 'Hanging Virgin' finally fell in March, 1918, after nearly three years of precarious suspension. It was restored to its position aloft the basilica of Notre Dame de Brebières after the War.

We circled over Péronne at 800ft, seeing clearly the Officer's Club and garden with its dilapidated ornamental architecture — the scene of our recent wearisome travels. Tomorrow we are to attempt to clear the enemy right out of the sky. We are to be over Busigny exactly 1¼ hours after take-off, at which time there will be twelve Camels at 15,000 and eighteen SE5As at 16,000 in the vicinity, waiting to pounce on the Hun and bag the lot if possible. Let us hope it comes off all right.

18 March
A perfect morning. I led off seven bombers and two fighters at 9.45 am and we all crossed the Lines in good formation over Bellicourt at 15,500ft. Above Beaurevoir Wodehouse, who was flying high, left the formation and turned back. Approaching Bohain the sky ahead seemed literally full of aircraft, three large formations of some twenty each to our north, and many smaller formations all about our height — but then too far to distinguish as friend or foe. Immediately after dropping our bombs and turning for home, every aircraft in the sky seemed to come together and there was a colossal mix-up. Everyone computed the enemy strength at between 50 and 60, and we ourselves numbered 38.

All engaged in a furious mêlée and immediately there were some fifteen or more Albatros and Fokker Triplanes on to our formation, very well handled, being part of the 'Richthofen Circus'.

At least 30 of the enemy were indeed from *Jagdstaffeln* 6, 10 and 11, led in person by Manfred von Richthofen.

I kept our formation together as far as possible and together we accounted for three — two certainties and one probable.

Things happened so quickly and the fight was on such a big scale that it was impossible to follow all that was happening, but we saw numbers of Huns spinning down and on fire, our Camels following them right down; also a few of our own out of control. I had my front guns on to an Albatros at about 30 yards range for a few seconds as he cut across our bows, and got some 20-30 rounds into him, but he dived, coming up again under our tail. I slewed enough for Naylor to get a long burst into him and he went down pouring black smoke from his tail. Meanwhile I was trying to keep count of our formation and saw what appeared to be one of our DHs at the rear gliding down trailing a column of black smoke. McBain's gunlayer, Jones, shot the tail off an Albatros and Dickson's got another down out of control.

Was this the one mentioned by Watkins? 'One Bosche triplane, painted all colours, got right in front of me, but I couldn't fire as Dixon was just in front of him. I saw him look round and catch sight of me, whereupon he slewed off right and was promptly bagged by an SE alongside me.'

We left the SEs and Camels still scrapping furiously, our instructions being to return immediately after dropping. Apart from accurate AA near the lines, our troubles were over.

This must have been the greatest aerial battle of the war so far, a total of nearly 100 aircraft engaged. On landing, found Wodehouse had been shot to blazes, being hit three times in the ankle and another in his left shoulder after penetrating his tank, none of them serious, however, and he pulled off a good landing with a seized engine in a field near the aerodrome. His machine was riddled, but his gunlayer, James, escaped with nothing worse than ripped clothing. Ransford failed to return and it must have been him we saw gliding down smoking badly. A sad loss and an excellent gunlayer in Smith. That makes our ninth casualty in nine consecutive days. The SEs accounted for eight Huns for the loss of two of their own, and the Camels for two certainties; but as five Camels who followed their quarry right down failed to return, they probably got several more. I was talking over the 'phone to Captain Kitto, 54 Squadron's leader, after we got back, and he said it was by far the biggest scrap he had ever been in. He seemed quite unnerved and kept repeating, "frightful affair, frightful affair." Undoubtedly the Germans accepted yesterday's challenge and concentrated their forces, including Richthofen's startlingly-coloured 'Circus' with the idea of annihilating us, but they suffered more than we did, despite the enormous tactical advantage of fighting many miles behind their own Lines. Many of them were really full-out and put up a good show, particularly the Fokker Triplanes*. The Colonel came over after lunch and discussed tomorrow's show, his idea being finally to smash up these big bands of Huns in one huge aerial battle. He proposes putting up some 60 fighters, we ourselves being used as bait once more – though I really don't think any bait is needed. However, this time we are not to go far over the Lines but, crossing three or four miles over up north, entice the enemy after us and draw him down south near St Quentin, where all our fighters will be hanging in the sun waiting for him and where his big advantage of his own ground will be nullified or considerably reduced. Very nice in theory – let's hope it will work.

19 March

Rain at last which provides a welcome rest, but it is a pity that show can't come off. The enemy and our side were teed up for it and it would have been a thrilling spectacle if 60 of our fighters could have fallen upon the 'Red Baron' and all his crowd, but we of course might not have succeeded in drawing them into our territory and could have suffered heavy casualties in the attempt. Anyway there it is and we have a day off, thanks to the weather. After lunch the CO, Jobling and I drove into Amiens, stopping at Villers Bretonneux on the way to take particulars of 27 Squadron's oxygen apparatus, which was explained to us by George Chester. We explored Amiens cathedral, one of the finest I've seen with its enormous lofty nave and magnificent west front. We arrived back to find two new Flight Sub-Lieutenants, Heywood and Evans.

20 March

A very wet morning. Wing Captain Lambe arrived just after lunch to look over the station, and later Brigadier L. E. O. Charlton (known as 'Leo'), commanding our 5th Brigade, together with a Major General of Engineers, dropped in to have tea with us. They were most friendly and

*This was the machine flown by the Red Baron and his "Circus".

talkative and the old General gave us a lot of interesting information. After tea the CO, Lupton, Watkins and I walked through the village and explored the ruins of the church, ascending the tower and finding a good observation post halfway up the semi-ruined spire, which gave an excellent view of the surrounding country. Compston and Booker now have squadrons and the CO told me he had impressed my name on Lambe for one, but I am sceptical of it coming to anything in view of the imminent formation of the new Air Force. A huge strafe on all along the Lines this evening. A special telegram of congratulations from General Salmond on our stunt of the 18th and work during the last fortnight.

11

The Ludendorff Offensive — 1918

The bombardment that descended on the British trenches in the early hours of the morning of 21 March along a seventy-mile front signalled the start of the greatest battle of the war. The collapse of the Russian armies the previous October and the weakened state of the British after Passchendaele, with the French torn by recent mutinies, presented Germany with one last window of opportunity to destroy the British army before American forces arrived in strength and naval blockade further weakened their people's resolve. For the British it became 'The March Retreat'; for the Germans it was the *'Kaiserschlacht'* — the Kaiser's Battle.

A spring attack at some point had been foreseen, and its location correctly guessed, but Lloyd George, determined to thwart the unquenched offensive ambitions of Haig, and shocked by the blood-letting of Passchendaele, refused reinforcements from the considerable reserves at home. Would not the Americans come soon if only the armies stood on the defensive? To add to Haig's weakness, he was asked to take over twenty-five more miles of front from the French on his right. It was ironic that this sector, in front of the town of St Quentin, was just where the main thrust would develop. It was also the destination of 5 Naval, when, at Haig's request, the Squadron moved to Mons-en-Chaussée to join RFC squadrons on 8 March. Opposite them was the German 18th Army; to their left the British Third Army, and on their right the French, while General Sir Hugh Gough's Fifth Army to which they were attached, held the twenty-five-mile front on which the blow was about to fall.

Division after division was moving across Germany from the east, with nine fresh divisions moving into the St Quentin sector. Altogether in the seventy miles between Arras and the French were massed a million men against less than half as many British.

In the words of the Official History, 'With the coming of night on the 20th the mist thickened and gave the illusion that it muffled sound, for the German artillery fire had ceased. The unusual silence was oppressive and, with the fog, combined to produce an atmosphere of the macabre. At 4.45 am on 21 March, out of the mist, the crash came.'

To the author's account is appended a note on the situation each day as it developed.

21 March

Awakened at 4.30 am by terrific drum-fire and the bursting of shells all round us. They came screaming over about every 60 seconds and some were far too close for comfort. Being a former German aerodrome, the gunners know our range exactly, though firing blind due to thick fog which blanketed everything. They made extraordinarily good shooting, landing some 50–100 shells on and just around the station. While several of us were standing in the Mess doorway one screamed over our heads and burst just by Dickson's cabin some 50 yards away, throwing up a volcano of earth and stones which fell all round us. Another burst in the trench surrounding some of the men's huts, blowing one end to bits, though miraculously no one was hurt. From pieces of shell we picked up, much of the stuff was 9in. An amusing incident while we were being bombarded was a telephone call from HQ instructing our CO to take steps for the growing of vegetables on the station! Shortly afterwards the line was put out of action.

We were all by this time feverishly flinging gear together, preparing for immediate evacuation as soon as the fog lifted. We breakfasted off bread and butter and tea and lunched about 11 am on bully beef sandwiches in between throwing gear on to the lorries and dodging periodic shells. Fortunately, many of the latter were dud, and the mist held, or some of us would have been blown to bits with all our gear. As it was we were extraordinarily lucky to have no casualties — 35 Squadron RFC nearby had three direct hits on their hangars. At 1.35 pm the mist had lifted sufficiently, so ten of us (our sum total of aircraft) took off, dodging the many craters on the aerodrome, to bomb bridges over the canal between the north end of the tunnel and Honnecourt. I was leading and we got good results from 8,000ft. The German barrage was now bursting on a line just east of Roysel, halfway between Péronne and the former Lines. We returned to Champien aerodrome, just east of Roye. All the gear, or as much of it as could be moved, came on by lorry. We landed at 3.15 pm and, hastily refuelling and rearming, left at 5.30 pm and just succeeded in pulling off another raid in the same area before dark — not a bad day's work — two stunts and a move after being shelled out of bed at 4.30 am! A formation of twelve EA attempted to get on our tails this evening, but we kept them at bay and Naylor shot a Fokker Triplane down out of control. The CO and I dined at 80 Squadron RFC with Major Bell and a nice lot of RFC fellows. The rest dined at 79 Squadron RFC. The strafe is still raging terrifically despite our present 22 miles from the lines. Mons-en-Chaussée being only eight, and right in the centre of the push, we were bound to catch it and the Wing Commander seems very pleased at our escape, plus two raids.

With the experience of the Cambrai tank fighting in mind the British defences had been hastily re-modelled during the winter to provide elasticity. A scantily held 'trip wire' line lay in front of a 'battle zone' some 8,000 yards deep, studded with numbers of concrete 'redoubts' having all-round defence with primitive minefields, while further back were two more trench lines. Fog prevented the redoubts from giving mutually supporting fire and increased the sense of isolation of forward units. By evening the battle zone itself had been largely breached. Many British units surrendered without a fight when they found themselves surrounded.

22 March

Thick fog again early, thank goodness. We are in very cramped quarters here, all officers sleeping and messing together in one long hut and the men in a Bessoneau, but how lucky to have any cover under these circumstances — compare the lot of the PBI. It cleared after lunch and ten of us took off at 2.30 pm, our target again being the canal bridges which are now some eight miles the wrong side of the Lines. However, we met with little trouble beyond some fair AA, though we saw a large formation of EA 2,000ft below. We landed at 4 pm and at once rearmed and left at 5.15 pm to bomb transport, enemy troops, batteries and in fact anything we could find in the neighbourhood between Roisel and the canal. We dropped our bombs on hutments and other buildings at Villeret and on transport at Templeux. The Germans are now on the outskirts of Roysel, reported to be in Ham and pushing steadily forward all along the line. We landed at 6.40 pm — I led both raids.

Pretty well the whole of the 22nd Wing have now moved on to this station, Nos 23, 48, 54 and 84 Squadrons RFC, as well as ourselves, the enemy being within two miles of Guizancourt when they left. Two of their motorcyclists, who had been sent out along the road armed with rifles to give the alarm as soon as the enemy appeared over the ridge, shot down a low-flying Albatros and took the pilot prisoner — an extraordinary piece of work. Many officers of 48 and 84 came in and dined with us, having no facilities themselves. Dad Weaver who went over to Mons to collect the remainder of the gear came back with the news that the Bosche were now within two miles of our old aerodrome and that the roads were one solid block of our troops and transport retreating pell-mell. Artillery are encamped on the aerodrome which is likely to be taken at any time. Drummond is in charge there, ready to fire the Bessoneaux and destroy everything at the last moment.

General Gough's Fifth Army were now retreating over open ground. The last reserves had been thrown in, and a critical situation arose in front of

St Quentin. It was now essential to try to reform behind the Somme to protect Amiens, only 30 miles from the sea.

23 March

A day of intense activity during which we pulled off four raids, three of which I led. On our first, leaving at 8.51 am, we straddled hutments and other buildings at Villers, our bombs falling in the target area. On the second at 11.25 am we obtained very good results on buildings, the railway sidings and junction at Roysel and Vendelles. The third, at 2.26 pm, saw good results at Tincourt and Marquaix, and on the fourth at 4.59 pm, over transport on the main road just east of Mons-en-Chaussée. The moment we landed after each raid, mechanics and armourers were round refuelling and rearming and we were off again after half an hour's rest, plus any refreshment we could get. Returning from our third raid I spotted an enemy two-seater on its back in a field just off our aerodrome and circled round it at 200ft. The pilot and observer were being led away. A couple of 23 Squadron's Spads had forced him to land.

The Germans are now across the Somme in several areas and we packed all our gear during a short lull at lunchtime. On our last raid we left with instructions to land at Bertangles – five miles north of Amiens. My engine started seizing up on the way back and I had to forceland at Villers Bretonneux. Despite my signals, half the formation followed me down and I had to push them off again for Bertangles under Watkins' lead. George Chester came out to me on the aerodrome and arranged for my old N6000 to be looked after. As they couldn't provide any transport, being under orders to move at any moment, I dined in 27 Squadron's Mess and got a shakedown in George's hut, 'The Casino' but I hardly slept a wink what with discomfort and cold, there being no heating of any sort, nor mattress or bedding. I was also very tired after four raids plus a move and no proper meals. Guns thundering furiously all day.

A three-mile gap had now opened between the British Third and Fifth Armies in the Peronne area. This is where 5 Naval made four raids, dropping 464 25lb and 20 112lb bombs on the attackers.

24 March

27 Squadron left on a raid to Valenciennes at 7.30 am. I breakfasted at 9 am and impatiently awaited transport and fitters from Bertangles, but I waited in vain and at 5 pm accepted Colonel Bolling's (USAS) offer to drive me over to Bertangles. It was a grilling hot day – it might have been July. He is himself staying in Amiens. The roads were choked with

transport and the railway one long chain of trains, many of them Red Cross. The Colonel insisted on filling up with a case of Burgundy and several pots of jam in Amiens for the cheering of our Mess. We arrived to find a somewhat chaotic state of affairs, little cover for any of our aircraft and all the ratings sleeping in the hangars and messing in the open. We ourselves have a Mess which is something to be thankful for, and are sleeping under canvas. I am in a tent with Toby Watkins. Our Colonel (of the 22nd Wing, F. V. Holt) stopped to dinner. He is an awfully good sort and a type to get things done whatever the difficulties. Rumours galore as to the enemy's progress.

The Germans were now thrusting towards Albert. Haig's Special Order of the Day to all ranks announced, 'We are again at a crisis in the war.'

25 March

Had a capital night, thank goodness — I needed it! This is a glorious spot, if only we can stop here. Lovely hilly and wooded country. Bertangles itself is a charming village on the edge of a wood which surrounds a wonderful old château. From the aerodrome it looks like a peep of Kent at its prettiest and, in the opposite direction, one sees Amiens Cathedral standing up majestically. All around is the most delightful open country to explore. As it is I expect we shall be retreating further west in a day or two.

I led off B Flight at 9.15 am on A8071, N6000 being out of action, to bomb anything of importance east of the Somme, along which we are holding the enemy for the moment in certain areas. A and C Flights are following half an hour later. The haze was so thick that one could only dimly spot woods and roads and, for a while, I could pick up no landmarks though I had a good idea of my whereabouts. Then I spotted the horse-shoe wood and got my bearings at once. Crossing the Somme just south of Brie, Naylor pulled off our bombs over transport and huts at Tertry, much to my disgust as I was steering a good line for our own and 35 Squadron's old aerodrome at Mons, where I had observed the Germans had already installed themselves and erected some twenty half-moon tents. Five Hun scouts took off from Mons just before we reached it. We landed shortly after 10 pm and pushed off again at 11.30 with a strong wind blowing from the north and thick clouds coming up. Through the clouds at 2,000 and I managed to pick up the horse-shoe wood through a gap and from that the Amiens-Albert road. Then with the aid of my compass and occasional glimpses of the country below, held a straight course for our objective, the Bapaume-Péronne road where the enemy is trying desperately to effect a breakthrough and has already reached Martinpuich and Flers. Albert was completely hidden but I spotted one of the Poizières mine craters which put me on my course for Bapaume, where we were fairly heavily 'archied.' We off-loaded our bombs over transport near Raincourt. Almost immediately on turning south, we were over Péronne, the wind drifting us down at an incredible speed. I picked up the St Quentin-Amiens road and, diving through the clouds, crossed the Somme just east of Amiens and so home. The bumps flying at 1,000ft were terrific and the bus out of control at times. A and C Flights got utterly lost on their second raid and found themselves drifted over Champien, not allowing sufficiently for the very strong north wind and seeing little of the ground owing to clouds and thick haze.

Rochford of 3 Naval landed at Bertangles at 2 pm with his Camel badly shot up from the ground over Le Sars at 500ft. He saw our troops in disorderly retreat in that neighbourhood. Things look pretty black and it seems likely the Germans may be in Amiens very soon. Villers Bretonneux has been evacuated in a great hurry. Watkins fetched my 'B1' (N6000) from there this morning. Much material was left behind and destroyed. I expect we will be clearing out of this nice spot at any time, which will make the third move in five days and the seventh since the squadron left Dunkirk nineteen days ago. After tea the CO, Watkins and I walked out towards Vaux through the fields — delightful country.

By now the Fifth Army was in collapse and was placed under the command of the French on its right, Gough being relieved. The separation of French and British armies was threatened, and Pétain talked of withdrawing in the direction of Paris on his own.

26 March
The weather which had rather raised our hopes of a quiet day dashed them again this morning with a clear sky and fresh north-east wind. A and C Flights left at 8.30 am and B Flight at 9.30 to bomb enemy transport etc on the roads between Bapaume and Albert, where the enemy is pressing violently and we are at present holding him on the line of the Ancre and along the Albert-Bray road. We got good results in the region Poizières-Pys-Courcelette-Le Sars-Flers area. We left again at 11.30 am for the Somme bridges at Brie, St Christ, Pargny and Bethencourt. My engine cut out on six cylinders over Querrieu and I had to drop out, Watkins taking over the lead. 'B1' (N6000) is evidently not yet recovered from her seizure on the 23rd. Pushed off on a third stunt at 2.30 pm. I steered a course over Péronne and Mons and then drifted rapidly down over the Somme, bombing transport at Voyennes

and around Nesle. Large cumulus clouds made observation difficult. I led off B Flight's fourth stunt at 5.20 pm. Mason and Carroll dropped out early. I took the formation round Roye and then beat up into the very strong north wind over our old aerodrome at Champien, on which we launched off four of our bombs, the remaining eight over transport on the Roye-Nesle road. The AA was very heavy and accurate. On the return journey I observed a colossal explosion in the neighbourhood of Ribemont, an enormous red sheet of flame, followed by a huge mushroom of smoke rising to fully 10,000ft. So finished a pretty hard days work, each formation completing four raids, making eight in all. Sixteen raids for practically every pilot in the last six days, ie since the push started. Special messages of congratulation for the squadron from General Sir Hubert Gough, commanding the 5th Army, and from the Admiralty. A priceless night with a full moon, consequently many EA around.

The remnants of the Fifth Army were ordered to hold the approaches to Amiens at all costs, but the gap before the city was widening owing to the precipitate retreat of the Third Army's 7th Corps on its left. Only 300 men of a scratch force (Carey's Force) and 50 machine gunners could be found to plug it. Foch became Allied C-in-C, after hints that Pétain might retreat. The Germans had brought up nine fresh divisions to this sector in the two previous days, and all squadrons were ordered to attack a huge concentration west of Bapaume, 5 Naval exploding an ammunition dump at Pozières. About this, a German officer recorded, 'At Pozières station on our left hostile airmen had bombed and set fire to several trains containing ammunition and supplies; continual heavy explosions could be heard which destroyed one wagon after another.' Later in the day they caught German infantry batallions de-bussing.

In the words of another pilot, Toby Watkins, sharing a tent with the author, he was 'More dead than alive by evening, could scarcely get out of machine. Food is nearly as scarce as sleep – but no one thinks of giving up.' The same pilot said, 'The country presents an extraordinary sight from above – columns of dense smoke going up to 8,000ft from nearly every town and village – enormous fires from burning stores and dumps – shells bursting every few yards – columns of our troops retreating along all main roads and stragglers tramping westward across the fields.'

27 March

We were called at 6.45 am for a stunt on the Somme bridges, now 10–12 miles behind the Lines. Misty and thick clouds at 1,500ft so I told Goble that conditions were hopeless for such a mission. He agreed so we turned in for another hour. We all left at 10.30 am however to bomb and shoot up enemy transport in the Chuignes-Dompière-Foucaucourt area, aircraft leaving individually to select their own targets. I crossed over Raincourt at 2,000 and we bombed long lines of transport on the road to Fontaine from 1,000ft, with great effect. We then shot up troops, transport and kite balloons for all we were worth. I got several bursts into a KB which was hauled down, and others into troops and transport from 800ft. Naylor fired 800 rounds with his back guns, getting a long burst into a grey and green Albatros just below us and saw him crash in a field. He also dispersed a machine-gun crew who were firing at us. In fact tracers had been streaking up at us from the ground for some time. Only after circling and diving low for fifteen minutes and exhausting our ammunition did we turn for home. Altogether a priceless stunt and a thrill to see the war from close range. Lupton got shot up by three Triplanes but forced one to land — 47 holes in his aircraft!

Watkins, on the same raid wrote, 'We've been ordered to adopt new tactics which frighten me stiff.' Contact patrols on scouts is highly dangerous work. On DH4s it's suicidal. We had to fly below 1,000ft on our three raids today, bombing and shooting up transport, troops and batteries, two or three miles behind the lines. We passed our scouts shooting up the trenches from our side of the Lines with no Hun scouts or Archie to worry them. Dropped my bombs from 900ft on transports, then flew up the road to let my gunlayer fire his two guns at columns of troops coming up as supports. Could see the Huns scattering to roadside and their machine gunners getting busy on me. Little holes began to appear in my planes (could hear the "Zipp" every time the machine was struck), so zoomed up to 2,000ft having first dived on machine guns' crew and dispersed them with a burst from my front gun. Then attacked a kite balloon, (none of ours were up, whilst theirs were strung up in rows quite close to the Lines). Got about ten rounds in when front gun jammed. Gunlayer had used up nearly all his ammunition so turned for home, leaving the kite balloon to Bartlett, who had just turned up. Bartlett got 50 rounds into KB as it was being hauled down, when nine Huns (Triplanes and Pfalzs) dived onto his tail. He saw them just in time and managed to get back with quite a lot of his bus undamaged.

We all left again 1.30 pm with similar and individual objectives and achieved equally good results. Three Triplanes dived on me near Fontaine after I had made several dives on a kite balloon and forced them to pull it down. Both Naylor's rear guns were jammed so I had to dive for the Lines, which I crossed very low down at 180mph. I then circled for some time over our own field gun and howitzer batteries near Harbonnières watching their fire and enemy shells falling around them. From 2-300ft one got a healthy bump if directly overhead. I observed movements of all sorts; gun limbers tearing about, ammunition being hurried up, men and horses on the run, ambulances and transport of all kinds in continuous streams on every road, and troops resting in the fields a mile or two behind the Lines. Also innumerable fires, ammunition dumps going up in colossal explosions and much else of interest. One enormous explosion, with a huge burst of flame some 500ft up in the air, was followed by a column of yellow smoke whose mushroom top merged quickly with the clouds.

We left for a third stunt in the same region at 3.20 pm and got heavily and accurately shelled at 2,000ft over Raincourt and had to weave and dodge continually. We dropped our bombs with good effect on transport and a battery at Chuignes. Numerous Huns about and Naylor was busily engaged so I didn't circle round shooting up the roads for long. Our men still hanging on in the same lines and I again watched battery play around Harbonnières and Caix. When over the former place, nine Huns suddenly appeared overhead and, our guns jamming after 60 rounds, we beat a retreat. The enemy seem to have quickly got effective AA into position – it was both plentiful and accurate. An enormous blaze accompanied by a huge pall of black smoke observed close to Raincourt. Dickson's observer, Scott, got a Hun down in flames and an Armstrong Whitworth of ours was seen to go down with its wings folded back.

> Watkins adds in his diary: 'I was flying up the Amiens-St Quentin road at about 1,000ft, after dropping bombs, firing at troops, etc, when I saw a formation of Hun Triplanes coming down nearly vertically on to me. Got off about 50 rounds at the leader and was beginning to say my prayers when I saw an enormous plume of black smoke from a burning dump drifting towards the Lines, so immediately camouflaged myself in this and got safely back at about 800ft. Lupton was unlucky enough to meet this same formation and was chased back three miles at 100-50ft, getting 46 holes, mostly from explosive bullets, in his machine and tank.'

The German Lines now run along the line of the Ancre, through Albert which is still being fiercely contested, past Morlancourt and Chipilly, Proyart, Raincourt, Vauvillers, Bouchoir and Guerbigny, down to Beauvraignes where the French are holding – as recorded in my operational map which accompanies me in the air and which I keep up to date from day to day. Our old aerodrome at Champien is now ten miles behind the Lines, and Mons fifteen. We now total thirteen raids in the last four days and many individual roving missions. Since their arrival on the Somme on 6 March, the squadron has now carried out some thirty raids in all and we are told that we hold the record for daily total of bombs dropped of any squadron in the Air Services. So the prestige of the RNAS is being upheld. Stocker, with Rendle, failed to return from our third mission. An Armstrong Whitworth of 35 Squadron nose-dived into the ground with bombs this evening and blew up, nothing being found of the pilot or observer. The CO, Watkins and I went into Amiens at 6.30 pm for half an hour. We found the place absolutely deserted, all shops shut and scarcely a civilian to be seen. It was heavily bombed last night. A large bomb was also dropped in the middle of 84 Squadron's aerodrome, some 500 yards from us.

The Germans were now able to exploit the gap between the British and worked round behind the Fifth Army, which utterly weary, held out magnificently. All air attacks concentrated on low-level and, for the bombers, highly dangerous strafing.

28 March

Clouds at 3,000 and strong south-west wind, nevertheless we all pushed off at 10 am on individual missions in the Dompière-Foucaucourt area. Crossed the Lines at 2,400ft near Raincourt and, within a minute, had eight EA round me. I dived on a yellow Pfalz* and drove him down; it then being altogether too hot I made for the Lines, leaving it to Naylor. He got one of the remaining seven down out of control, and two Fokker Triplanes converging on our tail collided and went down locked together, bursting into flames on the ground. Diving at 180mph, we outpaced the remaining Triplane and three Halberstadts and crossed the Lines. We had at any rate accounted for two, if not three, certainties and one possible out of eight, though I rather think the yellow Pfalz was a decoy with the other seven waiting up above to pounce as I dived on him. Naylor had not had a chance to unload his bombs so, after calming down a bit on our side of the Lines, we recrossed and, diving down, bombed transport on the road near Proyart. We didn't hang about looking for further trouble but on our way back observed that our field guns had withdrawn from Harbonnières to the woods just north of Villers Bretonneux aerodrome and our heavies are along the roadside at Fouilley.

* A well-streamlied monocoque fighter of which there were over 400 at the Front at this time.

We loaded up and left again at 11.45 am to bomb Cerisy pontoon bridge which the Germans had flung across the Somme. We made two runs over the bridge, our two 112lb bombs falling each side of it but no direct hit. AA was very heavy and also machine gun fire from the ground, tracers streaking all round. I circled for some time watching movements and, seeing three suspicious-looking aircraft near Bayonvillers, investigated and found them to be enemy two-seaters. I dived and got in a good burst at one and Naylor saw him go down and land in his own Lines. The other two beat it, keeping up a running fight with their rear guns. Trails of tracers all over the sky between us but we didn't allow ourselves to be drawn too far into their own territory. I landed at 1pm and was met with enthusiasm as several of our DHs had reported seeing a direct hit on me by AA and the machine falling in fragments. They had all met with terrible AA and seeing a direct hit concluded it was me as I was very late in returning. Poor Carroll and Duffy failed to return and we now conclude it must have been them. We are moving again and all our gear has already gone on.

The others left on a stunt at 3 pm but I, having gone very deaf, led our three new pilots, Cox, Day and Heywood, to our new aerodrome at Yvrench, north-east of Abbeville. Very windy and terrifically bumpy, almost completely out of control at 100ft going in to land and only just pulled out with my engine. On landing discovered it was 48 Squadron's aerodrome, our own being some two miles distant. Just after landing all our other aircraft arrived and landed on 23 Squadron's aerodrome across the road. Both aerodromes most fearful surface with holes and undulations, and how our eleven DHs managed to land and take off again with nothing worse than a broken propeller when Heywood's DH tipped onto its nose in a two-foot hole is a marvel. Our own aerodrome is only slightly better but it also abounds in large holes and depressions. After all, these emergency landing grounds are nothing more than large and often rough fields — the best that can be found for the purpose. Our only quarters at present are fourteen bell tents and one marquee, which tonight is used as Mess for officers and stewards, and sleeping quarters for gunlayers. The narrow road is blocked with transport and the lorry with all the officers' gear and bedding has broken down and is ditched many miles away. To add to our joy it started raining hard at 4 pm. We had a picnic supper and at last our gear turned up at 11 pm and we had a rare time sorting it out in the rain and getting our tents fixed up for the night.

The 28th marked the end of the critical phase and the consolidation of the Amiens defence line. 5 Naval dropped 3½ tons of bombs on the head of the German advance in front of Amiens.

29 March, Good Friday

Half a gale blowing all day, nevertheless the Colonel was anxious for us to push off on a raid. The CO, however, was firm — it would have been madness to fly a DH with full bomb load in such weather. Gamon, Lupton, Watkins and I went into Abbeville after tea in the CO's car, several others following in the tender. A not uninteresting town with a fine cathedral and west front but the interior is disappointing. Dined at the officers' club, getting back at 10.30 pm.

30 March

I led a formation of nine at 8.30 am to bomb the Somme bridges, but thick clouds at 3,000 made this impossible so we attacked transport on the road east of Bayonvillers. One of my 112lb fell in the middle of the road, making a huge crater and scattering transport in every direction, whilst the other was just off the road. About a dozen Triplanes and Pfalz scouts suddenly made an appearance but didn't seem over-anxious to close with us, contenting themselves with loosing off at long range. We patrolled up and down just our side of the Lines and watched old man Hun doing likewise in large numbers a mile or less away. After a number of dives to shoot up Lamotte and the main St Quentin-Amiens road, seven EA suddenly appeared above me which I recognized as Pfalz and so beat a retreat as Naylor's guns had jammed. The seven were reinforced by another formation of five and followed me back to the outskirts of Amiens but kept just below the clouds, ready to dodge into them if they met trouble. Made me wild that there were none of our fighters around. They certainly were none of Richthofen's crowd or they would have had me cold. As it was, by diving low I was safely away from them.

All 25 Squadron's Bessoneaux at Villers Bretonneux are destroyed but not 27 Squadron's. The enemy front line now runs from west of Albert, crossing the Ancre and the Somme, through Le Hamel and just east of Villers Bretonneux, then south-west to Moreuil and down to a few miles west of Montdidier I watched our batteries in action around Villers Bretonneux. There appears now to be no trench system between there and Amiens, the enemy having broken through the strong defensive line two or three miles east of Villers Bretonneux. I could see nothing between him and Amiens but a few isolated slit trenches. Stringer, Gamon's observer, shot a Fokker Triplane down and saw it crash. We were to have left again for the same locality, escorted by four SE5As, with the object of cleaning up some of the many EA we have seen, but rain set in. Heywood failed to return but news came through later that he had landed at 101 Squadron's aerodrome.

31 March
The CO left early for Dunkirk to see Wing Captain Lambe, leaving me in charge. I sent off a raid at 9.30 am, which Lupton led, all returning at 10.30 am. I led another at midday, Lupton, Gamon, Mason, Jolly and myself. Large cumulus and storm clouds but we managed to strike a channel and steer clear of most of them and our formation kept well together. I picked up the Somme, caught a glimpse of part of Amiens and then a short stretch of the Amiens-St Quentin road, finally sighting the German advanced landing ground between Caix and Rosière. Getting a good line, our two 112lb bombs fell one on the aerodrome amongst a group of twelve aeroplane tents and the other on the road which was packed with transport. Two of our aircraft failed to spot the aerodrome, which showed up well with its twelve white tents. Heavy storms in the afternoon prevented further operations. The CO returned at 7 pm with plenty of good news. Lambe could hardly say enough in our praise which, considering his usual reticence, is saying a lot. He has sent an account of our doings round to all the squadrons in his command, adding that if they can do half as well they may be proud of themselves!

1 April
We are the RNAS no longer. 5 Squadron RNAS has now become 205 Squadron, RAF and we adopt army ranks of Major, Captain and Lieutenant. I led off the first formation of nine at 9.20 am to bomb the bridges at Brie and St Christ. We crossed the Lines over Moreuil at 9,000 but were so heavily and accurately shelled, and threatened by innumerable EA with no fighter protection ourselves, that I decided to attack again Caix aerodrome and Rosières. Our two 112lb fell in the middle of Caix village which was again congested with transport. There were several hits on the aerodrome, but no direct hits on the aeroplane tents. We drove one EA down. I broke up the formation over Villers Bretonneux and descended to 800ft along the Lines near Berteaucourt and Domart, just north of Moreuil, where very great activity was in evidence. Large numbers of EA at 2,000ft just their side of the Lines, with which we had several long-range engagements. I fired some 200 rounds into a KB which was quickly hauled down.

Dickson led off a second raid at 1.45 pm and I left in the CO's car at 2.30 pm to discover what had become of Heywood who landed at 101

Squadron's aerodrome two days ago, but of whom we have had no further news. I was told they were at Fienvillers, south-west of Doullens, but on arrival found several other squadrons, but not 101. Our 1 Squadron (now 201) is there and I had tea with them, meeting Booker (now CO), Ridley, Rowlet and Magor whom I had not seen since Chingford days. I also found Cartmel, just discharged from hospital and awaiting transport, so brought him back with me. I eventually found 101 at Cote Vise, north of Coullens, but Heywood left there yesterday afternoon – goodness knows where he is now! Arrived back at 6.30 pm.

2 April
A very windy day with large cumulus formations. The RFC are sending their medical officers (MOs) round to former RNAS squadrons and they fastened on me as having been out too long and decided I must return home for a rest and then a spell of Home Establishment. I dare say they are right, though I hate the idea of saying goodbye to 205. These last three weeks have certainly been a bit strenuous. The CO, however, talks of my coming back with a squadron before long – may he be right! After lunch I led a formation of eleven on a further raid on Caix-Rosière aerodrome and village. A good formation despite the strong wind and clouds. John Gamon had to drop out at 8,000 with engine trouble. Good results as far as could be seen, but thick clouds made observation difficult. This was my 100th raid, including a few fighter patrols in my early days, and I have now been with the squadron for just over eighteen months. I would like to stay on and make it two years, especially as it seems we have now brought Ludendorff to a halt. His infantry have outpaced their supplies and he hasn't been able to get his artillery, especially the heavies, up quickly enough. It would be good to be with the squadron when we push forward again and re-occupy some of our old aerodromes.

After tea we left again for the Somme bridges, Lupton leading. We bombed Brie and St Christ bridges with fair success and, on our way back, I had a last exploration of the Lines around Moreuil and Demuin from 1,000ft. Still considerable activity and our heavies were firing furiously from the west side of the Noye River. A heavy storm threatening, so I beat it back to Yvrench. After dinner the CO forced me to get on my legs and make a farewell speech, which I did with fair success judging from the applause though quite unmerited. I just can't bear the thought of leaving the old squadron and such a grand lot of fellows. We have always been such a happy crowd in 5 Squadron, officers and ratings, and the way our fitters and riggers and armourers have slaved to keep us in the air during the last hectic weeks has been beyond praise. Later the CO, Watkins, Dickson, Luppy and I foregathered in John Gamon and Mason's tent and spent a jolly, and last, evening as far as I was concerned. Thank goodness dear old John is taking on B Flight. Watkins may be returning to Blighty with me.

12

A Casualty Fights Back

3 April

A wet morning spent mostly in packing and saying farewell to all the men in B Flight. I made a little speech and their affectionate farewells were really touching. Many requests to be in my squadron, if I ever get one, and there is not one of them I wouldn't gladly have. Petty Officers Clark and Langford, my chief fitter and rigger respectively, are both fine craftsmen, utterly reliable and inspire the very best from the men of the Flight. Langford, from one of our many split Clerget propellers, made me a magnificent prop boss clock holder with inlay mahogany face, mounted on a square moulded stand, faced in the centre below the clock circle with the most delicately cut representation of the 'albatros'*. A really fine piece of work into which I fitted a round French carriage clock obtained in Dunkirk. I knew nothing of it till the job was finished.

The Wing Commander was over in the morning and said a few rather gratifying words of farewell. The CO afterwards told me that both the Colonel and Wing Captain Lambe are recommending me for a squadron. He also told me that he had put my name in a second time for a Distinguished Service Order; all of which is very cheering, but it was with a heavy heart that I said goodbye to so many good friends, especially John [Gamon] and Luppy [Lupton], two of the best that ever were. We all mean to keep in touch and come together again some day if possible.

Watkins and I eventually got away at 3 pm and stopped at Conteville Château to pick up Leask and Travers of 84 Squadron who are also returning for a spell. Travers spun into telegraph wires near Villers Bretonneux getting away from four EA and escaped remarkably lightly from a very bad crash. We had tea before leaving the chateau and saying goodbye to Beauchamp Proctor**, Duke, Lister-Kaye and others. Our transport got hopelessly lost around Auxi-le-Château and we didn't reach 24 General Hospital at Etaples until 8 pm.

---

* Referring to the gilt badge worn by all RNAS pilots.
** Captain A. W. Beauchamp Proctor, VC, DSO, MC, DFC, 84 Squadron.

4 April

I was medically examined by Dr Corbett who decided I was run down and needed a rest, so I am for home in a day or two. Travers also comes with me, but Watkins and Leask are doubtful. In the afternoon I walked with Watkins to Paris Plage, meeting Leask and Travers on the way – a nice walk through pine woods.

6 April

Called in the middle of the night to catch the hospital train for Calais, which didn't leave until 3.30 am. Leask, Travers and Cunningham of 60 Squadron travelled with me, but poor old Toby Watkins is left behind. It took us five hours to reach Calais and then a wait of four hours on the hospital ship before we left, but at least we managed to get a decent breakfast. We finally reached Charing Cross at 7.30 pm and were driven in a private car to the London Hospital, after being regaled with coffee and biscuits and cheered by waiting crowds who flung flowers through the windows as we left. What impostors we felt, and how hard up some people must be for a job! Leask, Travers and I were put into the Charlotte Ward – everything very comfortable and a great improvement on 24 General. A nice staff of nurses who, I think, regarded us somewhat as frauds, having lost no limbs or otherwise been wounded.

10 April

Having obtained our leave warrants and spent a couple of days in town doing necessary shopping, lunching at the best places and doing a show, we went our separate ways. I to my home in Gloucestershire and then on with my people to Cornwall where at the Lizard we spent three delightful weeks exploring its glorious coastal scenery. After the tense, exhilarating atmosphere of the Somme, where each day was so full of excitement, interest and thrills, I found the quiet almost uncanny. It took a lot of getting used to and, at first, I found it in a way oppressive.

On the expiration of my leave I was posted to Prawle Point, at the extreme southern tip of Devon, to command an anti-submarine unit, equipped with the 230hp BHP-engined DH9. But I only lasted a week there before being shot into Stonehouse Naval Hospital at Plymouth. My tummy had been worrying me on and off for the last two or three months in France, but I kept going largely on excitement I suppose and now the reaction had set in and I found myself also in a state of feverish anxiety over everything. I was X-rayed and a major operation advised.

As the surgeon explained it to me, it all sounded eminently sensible and I felt that any positive action was preferable to continuing with the months of discomfort I had been enduring. I think actually I was a good case to experiment on, it being at that time a rather novel operation. At any rate, I said go ahead and, though in the long run I think I've been none the worse for it, coming on top of a condition of nervous exhaustion, it put me out of action for a long time and was ultimately the basis of my being invalided out of the service. That invaliding I twice overcame, being finally retained on a permanent commission, but with a very low medical category which put paid to my prospects of promotion.

Whilst in Stonehouse Hospital I was notified of the award of a Bar to my DSC, which did something to cheer me, though I had rather hoped for the DSO which Goble had told me on leaving 205 that he had for a second time recommended me. Perhaps it is worth quoting here the citation of the award which appeared in the *London Gazette*, as demonstrating the length to which the people who write these citations can let themselves go! The last part of the citation was certainly news to me. The citation read as follows: "For conspicuous bravery and devotion to duty in carrying out bombing raids and in attacking enemy aircraft. On March 28th, 1918, he carried out three bombing raids. Whilst returning from one of these missions he was attacked at a height of about 2,500 feet by three enemy triplanes and five other scouts. One of these he drove down with his front guns, whilst his Observer shot down out of control a second. Observing that two of the triplanes were diving on him and converging, he side-slipped his machine away with the result that the two enemy machines collided and fell to the ground together, where they burst into flames. He has carried out very many bombing raids and brought down several enemy machines, invariably showing the greatest skill and determination."

A bit fulsome to say the least and nothing I wrote in my brief report on landing should have given licence to such a vivid display of imagination! I was indeed weaving and side-slipping and doing all I knew how to avoid the concentrated fire of a number of enemy fighters on my tail, but to suggest that my manoeuvring 'caused' the two aircraft to crash into one another is stretching it a bit too far. They were obviously so intent on getting me that they failed to observe one another − and so my gunlayer and myself were able to escape from a very tight corner. I am glad to say that my gunlayer, Naylor, was awarded a Distinguished Service Medal. He had carried out a great many raids with me, invariably showing great coolness and courage.

As soon as I was sufficiently recovered from the operation, I was transferred to the Royal Naval Auxiliary Hospital at Peebles, housed in the former palatial Peebles Hydropathic, set in the midst of lovely grounds and surrounded by a glorious countryside — the right atmosphere in which to convalesce. Whilst there my promotion to Acting Major came through, also a letter telling me that Goble was leaving 205 and asking if I was available to come out and take over the squadron. Unfortunately, I had to reply that I was still on the sick list. Less than a month later a second invitation came through but again and, most regretfully, I had to decline. I have often thought how different my future might have been had I been able to accept. Nothing would have given me greater joy than to have commanded the squadron throughout its recovery of the ground over which we had been so unceremoniously hustled back, and to have been with it up to the day of final victory. But it was not to be and I console myself with the thought that I might well have been dead!

Somehow, despite the lovely surroundings and pleasant company at Peebles, I didn't seem to make the full recovery hoped for and, after being in and out of convalescent homes and getting more and more depressed by them, I eventually persuaded the authorities to give me three months' sick leave to proceed to Switzerland and 'get away from it all'. Unfortunately that was not the end of it all, for on my way up to Les Avants, above Montreux, I was running a temperature and next day was down with 'flu, or *La Grippe*, as it was known out there, which was rampant throughout Europe in 1919. People were dying off like flies at Château D'Eux a few miles away, and here was I, having come out for a final recovery, laid up with a temperature of 104 degrees. After three weeks I was about again and, as by then the thaw had set in, I linked up with some nice French people and went down to Locarno which was looking lovely in the early spring. Whilst there, orders arrived for me to report to the Central Medical Board for examination and I regretfully left my nice friends, who told me of a good doctor and psychologist at Adelboden, should I need further treatment. Although a good deal fitter, I was still not 100 per cent but felt I had turned the corner and reached the stage where I should begin to pick up.

Arriving at the Medical Board, I was put through the innumerable tests for flying fitness but was unable to 'blow the mercury high enough' 'hold my breath long enough' and 'stand on one foot with my eyes shut steadily enough' to pass, and though they were sympathetic having regard to my war service, there was apparently no option under the regulations but to recommend me for invaliding from the Service. This happened towards the end of July and, having been so impressed with all my friends had told me about the doctor at Adelboden, I determined to get out there and put myself in his hands, but finance was the difficulty and my service pay would soon be ceasing. So I went to see the then head of the British Red Cross and was able to satisfy her as to the likelihood of my recovery under Dr Schaer. She most kindly undertook to meet much of the expense and off I went straight away to Adelboden. I liked Dr Schaer from the outset and he was able to assure me that organically there was nothing wrong, but that I was suffering from the after-effects of complete nervous exhaustion, and he told me that before I left I would climb all the mountains in the district — and so I did. I told him I would want to climb the Matterhorn as soon as I saw it. He assured me I could do it and, before I had been at Zermatt a week, I had scaled its 14,800 odd feet with the aid of one guide who had hurried me up it, as, being late in the season, he was doubtful of the weather. My guide, Oscar Julen, who at that time had just been promoted from porter, went on to become a very famous Swiss guide and yet, ironically, met his death by falling off a ladder.

I now returned to England determined to defeat the medicos and, as a first step, presented myself for examination for a civil pilot's licence. Having passed that all right I went to see Air Transport & Travel, the forerunner of Imperial Airways, but they told me there was little prospect at the time in civil aviation and advised me to try and get back into the RAF. So I again applied for examination by the Central Medical Board and, to the amazement of everyone there, blew the mercury sky high and passed all the other tests and, somewhat to my surprise, was reinstated in the RAF in my former rank, this after being invalided as 'permanently unfit as pilot or observer' six months before! All was well till I was posted to Baghdad with 30 Squadron early in 1922 when after six months, a week of 125 degrees in the shade and the electric fans having given out, I went down with heat exhaustion and spasms of appalling cramp. As soon as they got me into hospital and saw my medical history, they told me I should never have been sent to Iraq and posted me back to England with, to my dismay, a recommendation to be invalided for a second time.

I arrived back in September, just a year after my marriage, to see my two-months old son for the first time; separation after only four months of married life had been a severe wrench. Again I had to report to the medical board and this time was told that due to my prolonged period of high altitude flying — in those days in an open cockpit and without oxygen or any form of heating — I had gone past the breaking point and would never be the same again.

My father served another ten years in the RAF confined to ground duties, and did not take the controls again except as a glider pilot. As a fellow member of his squadron remarked, he seemed to lead a charmed life at a period in the War when the life of a pilot was reckoned in days, and he lived on to the great age of 98. His apotheosis came in his eighties when he was invited to be the guest of the RAF in Singapore for the disbandment ceremonies of his old squadron which had operated as a maritime squadron in the Far East for 44 years. '5 Naval' had become 205, a flying boat and later a Shackleton squadron, and to the end retained its links with the sea.

THE GNOME & LE RHONE 110 HP ROTARY ENGINE
9 cylinder,4 stroke engine fitted to the
Nieuport and other early aircraft.

The weight of the rotating engine is
supported entirely on the crankshaft which
is integral with the airframe bearer plates.
There is no carburettor.Petrol is fed via
the crankshaft to the crankcase,where it
meets air taken through the propellor boss
and the front end of the crankshaft.The
explosive mixture is centrifugally expelled
via the induction pipes into the cylinder
combustion spaces.
Inlet and exhaust valves are worked by common
push rods from a cam ring which does not rotate.
Attached to the back of the crankcase are gear
rings for driving the lubricating oil pump
and the magneto,which supplies high voltage to
distributor segments on a ring attached to the
rotating crankcase.
The engine rotates in a cowling which also
serves in place of an exhaust manifold.
Engine speed was normally constant, but in some
engines could be controlled by varying the lift
of the exhaust valve.Oil consumption was very
heavy-about 2 gallons per hour,while freezing of
the mixture in the induction pipes could lead to
engine failure.

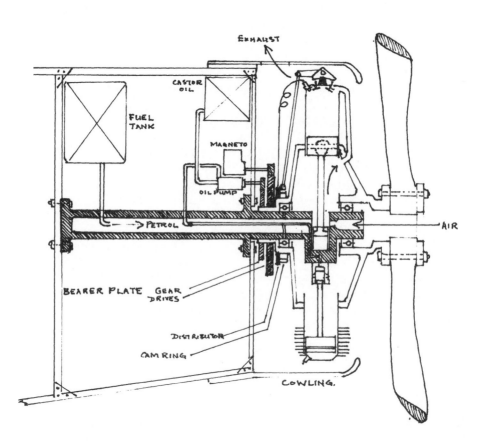

EXHAUST

CASTOR OIL

FUEL TANK

MAGNETO

OIL PUMP

PETROL

AIR

BEARER PLATE   GEAR DRIVES

DISTRIBUTOR

CAM RING

COWLING.

INDEX